*f*P

Daily Readings
from

Love Your Life

Devotions for Living Happy,
Healthy, and Whole

Victoria Osteen

FREE PRESS
New York   London   Toronto   Sydney

Free Press
A Division of Simon & Schuster, Inc.
1230 Avenue of the Americas
New York, NY 10020

For information about special discounts for bulk purchases,
please contact Simon & Schuster Special Sales at 1-866-506-1949
or business@simonandschuster.com.

The Simon & Schuster Speakers Bureau can bring authors to your live event. For more information or to book an event contact the Simon & Schuster Speakers Bureau at 1-866-248-3049 or visit our website at www.simonspeakers.com.

Manufactured in the United States of America

1   3   5   7   9   10   8   6   4   2

Library of Congress Cataloging-in-Publication Data
Osteen, Victoria.
Daily readings from Love your life : devotions for living happy, healthy,
and whole / by Victoria Osteen.
p. cm.
1. Christian women—Prayers and devotions.   2. Self-realization—
Religious aspects—Christianity—Prayers and devotions.
I. Osteen, Victoria. Love your life.   II. Title.
BV4844.O78   2011
242'.643—dc22   2010049242
ISBN 978-1-5011-0053-6
ISBN 978-1-4516-1041-3 (ebook)

Contents

Daily Readings
from

Love Your Life

Chapter One

Understanding Your Influence

Your Memory Box

As he thinks in his heart, so is he.
Proverbs 23:7 (NKJV)

If you're like me, you might have a special box filled with memorabilia. Maybe it has some cards or letters from a loved one, special photos, your kids' artwork, or ticket stubs from an important event. When I look through my memory box, it reminds me of where I've come from and connects me to what's most important in my life.

In the same way, every person has a memory box inside of her. You can choose what to place inside your memory box just like you would choose what to hold on to in the natural. Scripture says that what you put inside the memory box of your heart defines and shapes who you are and sets the course for your life. Your thoughts set you up to win or lose. If your memory box is filled with bitterness, unforgiveness, or negative attitudes, your life will follow a negative path. But when you fill your heart with the treasure of God's Word, you will be set free to live the life of blessing God has prepared for you.

Storing the right treasures inside of you doesn't just happen automatically. Many influences come against us, voices from the past, opinions of others, even images in the media. It takes effort to guard your heart and retrain your thinking. You are the one responsible for making sure that every time you go to your memory box, it is filled with the truth of God's Word to remind you of how valuable you really are. Doing so can be as easy as writing down a few scriptures on 3x5 cards and taking them with you everywhere you go. Or write down some things you are thankful for, and remind yourself of all the times God protected you and helped you overcome obstacles. When you rehearse over and over all the good things God has done in your life, you are retraining your mind and creating an internal foundation of strength and power.

Just like a great coach takes the time to build up his team and get them thinking in the right direction before the big game, you have to take time every morning to "coach" your thought life, too. You can't just wait to see how the day will unfold; you have to set yourself up for victory. Winning isn't just about ability; it's about attitude, mind-set, and internal dialogue. Believe that you are created to win because what you believe about yourself affects your future more than anything else. You have to see yourself as a winner before anyone else will. I encourage you to fill your memory box with the truth of God's word, which says, "You are more than a conqueror. You are equipped. You are well able to overcome any obstacle you may face." See yourself as valuable and victorious because a healthy self-image is one of the greatest assets you can have.

Maybe it's been challenging to see yourself as a winner up until this point. Perhaps some unfair things happened in your past—you were wrongfully accused, lost your job, or someone walked out on you. If you hold on to the past and keep those negative memories in your heart, they will weigh you down and prevent you from becoming all that God intends for you to be. Don't let what others have said or done stop you from living with purpose and enthusiasm! Nothing from the past can change your value in the eyes of God. Today is a new day, and now is the time to get a fresh, new outlook on life. It's time to clean out those negative memories and forgive those who have wronged you.

Today, take some time to examine the contents of your memory box. Are there any negative mind-sets that you need to change? Do you see yourself the way God sees you—as *valuable* and *important*? Look past whatever you may be feeling about yourself and focus on what God says about you. Remember, you are not here by accident. You are created in the image of Almighty God and your life is full of purpose. You are God's special treasure. No one can keep you from your destiny and nothing can disqualify you from your purpose.

Scripture Reading: Psalm 139:1–18

 PRAYER FOR TODAY

Heavenly Father, I humbly come to You inviting You to search and know my heart. I want to live a life that is pleasing to You and will fulfill my purpose. Search my heart and remove anything that would hold me back. Help me to forgive; help me to let go of the past. Create in me a clean heart and renew a right spirit in me as I set my thoughts on Your Word. Thank You for the good things You have in store for my future. In Jesus' Name. Amen.

You Are a Person of Influence

"Follow my example, as I follow the example of Christ."
1 Corinthians 11:1 (NIV)

Your purpose in this life involves more than just your own accomplishments and destiny; it also involves bringing good to others and adding value to the people around you. Whether you realize it or not, you are a person of tremendous influence. You are affecting the people around you even in the most subtle ways. You are setting standards and effecting change everywhere you go. Have you ever tossed a stone out into a lake or pond? Just like that stone sends out ripples across the water, your life "ripples out" and has increasing influence on those around you.

Influence is simply defined as the power to produce an effect without an apparent exertion. In other words, just by living your daily life, you are producing an effect. If you don't understand your full value and just live your life without focus or purpose, your example allows the people around you to rationalize living the same way. But if you go out determined to live at your best, you are raising the standard. You are being a leader and influencing others in a way that pleases God.

You are never too young and never too old to influence and inspire the world around you. Joel and I have done our best to instill this principle into our children at the very earliest age. We want them to know their value and to understand that they are an important part of everything we do. We want them to know that not only do they matter to us, they matter to God and they matter to the world around them.

When Alexandra was just five years old, she loved to sing, and her daddy loved to hear her sing. One day Joel asked her if she would sing a special song at the end of one of our worship events in another city, and Alexandra agreed. I was so proud of her and impressed by her confidence. Here she was just a little girl, standing up in front of thousands of adults, and she didn't appear to be nervous at all. She just stepped out on stage and did what she loved. She sang beautifully, and now she regularly sings when we go on tour. She is always such a blessing to the people in the service, but what amazes me most are the letters we receive from children and parents all over the country about how Alexandra's example motivates and inspires them. Children who used to be afraid to participate in a school or church program have been inspired by Alexandra's boldness and are now finding their own courage to step out as well. Alexandra was simply being herself, and if a five-year-old can influence the people around her by using her gifts and abilities, you and I can too!

You don't have to be on a stage or in front of a large crowd to make a difference; you are making a difference by living your life to the best of your ability. Remember, people are constantly watching and learning from your example—whether positive or negative. You may never know all the lives you are silently touching, so embrace the truth that you are important! Pen those words on your heart and hold them dearly to you, because the way you live your life matters. When you recognize your importance, you are honoring God and reflecting to others the value He has placed in you.

Scripture Reading:
Matthew 5:14–16; Colossians 3:15–17

⚬⚬⚬ PRAYER FOR TODAY ⚬⚬⚬

Heavenly Father, today I declare that I am a person of influence, chosen and equipped by You. Help me to recognize the opportunities You've ordained for me to be an example to others. Give me the boldness and wisdom to step out and shine in ways that honor You. Thank You for the destiny You have prepared for me and for setting me on the path toward success in every area of my life. In Jesus' Name. Amen.

You Are the Spice of Life

*A cheerful look brings joy to the heart, and
good news gives health to the bones.*
Proverbs 15:30 (NIV)

As the poet John Donne wrote, "No man is an island, entire of itself." Life is a group experience; we need people in our lives, and the people in our lives need us. Not only are you equipped with unique gifts and talents, but you have the power to lift the spirits of the people around you. You are the spice of life, created to bring zest and flavor to others just by being yourself.

Any good recipe requires seasoning. There's a popular television chef who shouts, "Bam!" every time he puts the seasoning in his dish that takes it over the top. Well, when you use your influence to lift the hearts of the people around you, you put the "bam" in life!

In our family, I tend to be the one who's always laughing about something and trying to find the humor in everyday life. One time, when we were all in the kitchen, I was making a joke about something that happened. Admittedly, it was a little corny. My teenage son, Jonathan, just rolled his eyes and shook his head but managed a big smile. (I could tell he wanted to laugh, though.) We all knew the joke was a bust, but Joel immediately piped up, "You know,

Jonathan, if it weren't for your mother, it would be pretty boring around this house." I took that as a huge compliment, because, of course, no one wants to live in a boring house!

Just by creating a lighthearted atmosphere, you can enjoy your relationships more and be more productive when you work together. A good sense of humor and a positive outlook can add so much value to the world around you. Scripture tells us that a happy heart does good like medicine, and a cheerful look can make a huge difference in others. Even God laughs in the heavenlies! When you keep things happy and light, you are opening the way for His healing power.

Think about the people you like to be around and do projects with. It's probably not the people who show up and constantly talk about their problems and how bad everything is, or the people who go on and on about how impossible things are or say that you'll never get the project done on time. When you're around those types of people, you can literally feel the life and energy being drained right out of you. But then there are those people who are always smiling, always encouraging, always looking for the good and bringing a "can do" attitude. Those are the "spicy" people. You feel empowered and strengthened around them, and those are the kinds of people we should aspire to be.

As you go about your day today, be conscious of the fact that you can make a difference in people by simply sharing a smile, a joke, or a kind word. Be the one who brings strength and joy in your relationships, on the job, in your family, and everywhere you go. You are the spice of life, and bringing flavor to others and lifting their spirits is the recipe for a happy, blessed, and prosperous life!

Scripture Reading: Ecclesiastes 4:9–12

PRAYER FOR TODAY

Father God, thank You for creating me in Your image with unique gifts and abilities to inspire those around me. Help me to see the humor in everyday life, to lift others' spirits and help lighten their loads. Thank You for filling me with Your joy, which is strength, and for empowering me to influence those around me for good today and every day. In Jesus' Name. Amen.

11

Stewarding Your Influence

"I will look on you with favor and make you
fruitful and increase your numbers,
and I will keep my covenant with you."
Leviticus 26:9 (NIV)

Everything we have in this life is a gift from God above, and we are called to be faithful stewards over the resources He's entrusted to us. The Bible says that when we are faithful over what He's placed in our hands, no matter how small it may seem, He will bless it and multiply it. In the same way, when we learn to steward the influence He's given us and use it for the benefit of others, He promises to increase it. He promises to pour out His blessing and favor upon us and make us fruitful in the earth.

I heard a funny story about a newly elected mayor of a town in Ohio. As he and his wife were riding in the motorcade of the inaugural parade down Main Street, waving to the crowds of people gathered along the route, they passed a man who was calling out to the mayor's wife. The mayor asked, "Who is that man?"

"That is my old boyfriend," his wife responded coyly.

The mayor nodded his head and said, "Just think; if you would have married him, you wouldn't be the mayor's wife today."

She smiled and answered, "No, if I would have married him, *he would be the mayor today.*"

Now, that's my kind of woman! She recognized her influence and knew how to use it for the benefit of others; the question for you is: Do you recognize yours?

Many people today think that in order to be influential, you have to have a powerful position or a large amount of money. But the truth is that influence isn't at all about a social position, a title, or a degree. In God's eyes, influence is about your heart condition. When you have a heart of excellence, a heart that goes above and beyond to do what is right, people take notice, and it affects them. Most important, God takes notice. That's the kind of heart God can bless and promote. That's the kind of influence He will multiply.

One of my favorite stories in the Bible is about a young girl named Esther. Esther wasn't born into privilege. In fact, she was orphaned as a young girl and seemed to have little hope for significance. But her attitude of excellence and her belief that she had a purpose greater than herself is what made all the difference. She was a steward of her influence, careful about the choices she made, and God entrusted her with tremendous favor. Because of God's favor on her life, she was positioned as queen, and she ultimately used her influence to save her entire nation from annihilation!

Today, God wants to crown you with His favor, just like He crowned Esther. He wants to position you in places that you never dreamed possible. But it all starts with your being a good steward of your influence and mindful of the example you are setting for others. Don't let the world around you influence your choices and standards; instead, you be the leader and set the standard. God has equipped you with power to overcome in every area of this life. He has deposited His wisdom in you, and He is ordering and directing your steps.

As you approach life with a heart of excellence and focus on living your best, God will multiply your influence and use you in ways you never imagined. Believe it today because His hand of blessing is upon you to accomplish everything He's placed in your heart!

Scripture Reading: Esther 2:1–9

⌘⌘⌘ PRAYER FOR TODAY ⌘⌘⌘

Father in heaven, thank You for choosing me for such a time as this. Thank You for looking upon me with Your favor, grace, mercy, and blessing. Help me see all the ways I impact others so that I can be a good steward of the influence You have entrusted to me. Show me Your ways, speak Your truth to my heart, and let everything I do bring honor to You. In Jesus' Name. Amen.

Look Beyond Your Limits

Surely the arm of the LORD is not too short
to save, nor His ear too dull to hear.
Isaiah 59:1 (NIV)

One day, during the prayer time in one of our church services, a woman came to me for prayer. She told me she had made some wrong decisions in her relationship with her grown daughter and that they were in strife and not talking to each other. The woman was so distraught, and it looked like there wasn't any hope for the situation in the natural. There seemed to be a mountain in between her and her daughter. As I listened to her story, I really didn't know what to pray, but as I started, I heard myself say something that I don't think I had ever said before. As I prayed, I said, "God, it looks like her hands are tied. There's nothing else she can do." Then something just rose up out of my spirit, and I said, "God, even though her hands are tied, I know your hands are not tied." As soon as those words passed my lips, something leaped inside of me and a light of hope shone on the woman's face. She immediately changed her focus and was filled with faith. She knew she didn't have all the answers, but she was able to look past her limits and open her heart to what God could do in her life.

You may be facing a situation right now where you feel like your hands are tied. Maybe the negative voices are constantly playing over and over, reminding you of how it's not going to work out, or how impossible things seem. It may be true that your hands are tied in the natural, and it's okay to admit, "My hands are tied." But always know that God's hands are never tied. With Him, all things are possible. He can do whatever is necessary to bring you through. His power is unlimited. Nothing is too difficult for Him.

Not only are His hands free to help you today, they are stretched out, inviting you to come and find rest for your soul. It doesn't matter what you've done; it doesn't matter how you ended up in the situation you're in. God's love knows no limits, and He is ready, willing, and able to help you today. In an instant, He can turn around any situation. In an instant, He can open up the right doors and cause the right people to show favor toward you. He can soften hard hearts and give you favor with the authorities. He can cause people to change their minds and want to bless you. You may not see a way, but God can make a way. Your job isn't to try to figure it all out; your job is to trust and believe Him, knowing that He is good and that you are a person of destiny, chosen and equipped for His purposes.

Today, I want to challenge you to look beyond your limits and consider what God can do in your life. No matter what may come against you, face it in faith and don't back down. His hands are never tied, and He is more than able to do the impossible in your life!

Scripture Reading: Mark 11:22–25

 PRAYER FOR TODAY

Heavenly Father, I come to You today, giving You all that I am. I release my cares and concerns into Your capable hands. I trust that You

are working behind the scenes, and even when I can't see a way, I know that You are making a way. Even when it seems that my hands are tied, I know that Your hands are never tied. Thank You for Your faithfulness to me, and thank You for strengthening me as I keep my heart and mind focused on You. In Jesus' Name. Amen.

Chosen and Equipped

You did not choose me, but I chose you and
appointed you to go and bear fruit.
John 15:16 (NIV)

One of the great stories in the Bible is about a shepherd boy named David, who defeated the giant, Goliath, with nothing but a single stone and a simple slingshot. Everyone marveled at David's boldness and ability to take on such a warrior, but it wasn't by accident that David had the confidence that he did. He didn't just wake up one day and decide to take out a nine-foot giant. He had plenty of opportunities to be discouraged and feel disqualified throughout his life, but instead he held on to the truth that he was handpicked by God and drew confidence from his past successes.

Long before David became the king of Israel, he spent his days looking after his father's sheep. His life wasn't the easiest. He had been overlooked by his father, criticized by his brothers, and regarded by many as just a shepherd boy. One time, the prophet Samuel went to David's house to choose who would become the next king. He asked to see all the brothers, but David's father was so certain that David, the youngest, wasn't a candidate for such a prominent position that he left him out working in the field. When Samuel didn't select any of the other seven brothers, David was

18

finally called in and was then anointed to be the future king of Israel. Even after that, David's family didn't seem to treat him any differently. They may have even thought Samuel had made a mistake. In fact, while David's brothers spent their time serving in King Saul's army, a prestigious position of honor, David was still the one doing the grunt work out in the shepherd's fields. He was seen as an errand runner, tasked with bringing lunch to his brothers, "the important ones."

One day while David was tending the flock, a hungry lion approached with every intention of dining on one of his sheep. Now we know from the Bible that David had a strong, abiding faith in God. He may have been young and inexperienced, and he may have been feeling fear when he saw the lion, but with God on his side, he overcame that lion. On another day a hungry bear approached, also intending to make a meal of David's sheep. Once again, David put his faith in God, killed the bear, and protected his flock. By the time David faced Goliath, he had already tapped into the strength and greatness that God had placed within him. David approached Goliath with confidence, knowing that with God on his side, he would have the victory.

But what if David hadn't faced the lion and the bear? What if he allowed the opinions of his brothers, instead of God's opinion, to define him? He might have gone around feeling insecure and questioning God. However, even though it seemed as if life had overlooked him, David knew he was *handpicked* by God. David chose to stand and believe no matter what his circumstances looked like. He was equipped through his past successes, and at the right time, he was promoted to be king.

Today, you may feel like an "errand runner" or that life has overlooked you. You've done your best, but maybe you haven't seen the results you anticipated. Or maybe you've been through some disappointments and now you're tempted to think, *Oh what's the use? I'll never get out of this situation. I'll never accomplish my dreams.* But don't believe those lies! God doesn't choose the equipped; He equips the chosen. Have confidence today because God has chosen you. You are *handpicked* by Him, and He who promised is faithful! When you go through setbacks or when people leave you out, remember, God is working behind the scenes. Stay in faith today, and keep moving forward one step at a time, because you are chosen and equipped to overcome every obstacle and live as royalty in this life!

Scripture Reading: Colossians 3:12–17

PRAYER FOR TODAY

Heavenly Father, thank You for choosing me. Thank You for equipping me to fulfill what You have placed in my heart. Today, I choose to trust You even when things don't go the way I planned. I choose to look beyond my feelings and, instead, look to You, because You are the author and finisher of my faith. Thank You for doing a good work in me. In Jesus' Name. Amen.

Applaud Yourself

The whole law can be summed up in this one command: "Love your neighbor as yourself."
Galatians 5:14 (NLT)

So often, it's easy to see the strengths and talents in other people, yet we tend to ignore the good qualities in ourselves. In fact, most people are their own worst critics, but really, we should be our own best cheerleaders! Of course this doesn't mean that we should be egotistical or boastful, but we should see ourselves the way God created us—as good—and we should learn to applaud even the little accomplishments in our lives.

Studies show that a negative attitude toward yourself not only sours your day-to-day life, but it actually hinders your personal growth. A negative attitude keeps you stuck. In order to move forward, you have to love yourself and accept yourself for who you are. After all, God does, and when you get into agreement with Him, you open the door for His power in your life.

One time I was on the treadmill at the gym having a conversation with a woman who had just been diagnosed with cancer. She asked me to pray for her and I said, "Yes, I will pray for you, but I have to tell you something first." Then, I looked her straight in the eyes and said, "You know, you ought to be so proud of yourself.

Look at you! You got up today and came to the gym. You could have pulled the covers over your head and stayed in bed, but you didn't. Instead, you are facing this with great hope and faith. I admire you, and you should applaud yourself."

When this woman was reminded of her own strength and tenacity, her whole demeanor changed. She had a big smile on her face and pulled her shoulders back as she recognized the importance of affirming herself and building herself up. I believe that in that moment, she saw herself the way God sees her which ignited her faith and renewed her hope. She saw the value in what she had done and she chose to applaud herself for it.

Not only can you applaud yourself with your words, but you can applaud yourself with your actions. I have found that the way we treat ourselves sets the example for how others will treat us. When you treat yourself as valuable, then others will recognize your worth and treat you as valuable, too. When you honor and value yourself, you are honoring God because you are His creation, a beautiful reflection of Him.

Carol was a bright, talented, and lovely young woman who experienced the pain of a broken relationship many years ago. As time passed, she was healing and growing stronger; however, as a single woman, she found Valentine's Day to be the hardest day of the year. It reminded her of her deep loneliness, and she would find herself in tears by the end of the day, longing to be loved. One year she decided she wasn't going to allow herself to fall into that cycle again. Carol decided that if there wasn't anyone to buy her balloons and roses, she would buy them herself. The night before Valentine's Day she went to the store, and since she couldn't decide on pink or red roses, she bought a dozen of each. She carefully displayed them in a vase on her desk, and the next day the office was buzzing. "Who bought you those gorgeous flowers?" people asked. "Oh, someone very special," Carol replied with a smile. For the first time, she truly saw herself as special, and the people around her did, too. That simple investment in herself filled a void that for many years had consumed her. She stopped looking outward and expecting others to meet that need for validation, and started showing love to herself. She honored herself and felt God honoring her, too!

Today, you may be going through a difficult situation, but be encouraged because you have strength inside to make it through. God has deposited seeds of success within you, and when you applaud yourself you are tapping into the greatness within. Start right now by reminding yourself of all the things you are doing right. Did you complete a project you'd been putting off? Applaud yourself. Were you nice to a difficult person in your life? Applaud yourself. Are you overcoming an addiction? Applaud yourself. You don't have to wait for other people to validate you. Know that God validates you, and because of that, you can validate and affirm yourself!

Scripture Reading: 1 Corinthians 13:4–12

PRAYER FOR TODAY

Heavenly Father, thank You for loving me. Thank You for giving me new life through Your Son, Jesus, and enabling me to walk in love. I receive Your love today so that I can learn to love others better. Help me to see the good in others and applaud them as I learn to see the good in me and applaud myself. I bless You today and always. In Jesus' Name. Amen.

Take Time to Receive

*Come to Me, all you who are weary and burdened,
and I will give you rest. Take My yoke upon you
and learn from Me, for I am gentle and humble
in heart, and you will find rest for your souls.
For My yoke is easy and My burden is light.*
Matthew 11:28–30 (NIV)

The Bible talks about two sisters, Mary and Martha. Jesus went to the house of these two sisters, and Mary chose to sit at His feet and receive from His teachings while Martha chose to work tirelessly to serve Him. She wanted everything to be perfect. Martha began to get frustrated because she was doing all the work and her sister, Mary, wasn't helping, so she said, "Jesus, could You tell Mary to get up and come help me? I mean, there's so much that needs to be done here, and I'm the one doing all the work." Now, how often do we have the same attitude Martha did? "Jesus, do You see how hard I'm working? Do You see how overwhelmed I am? Do You notice how much I'm doing for You?" I think Jesus would respond to us today in the same way He responded to Martha. In essence He said to her, "Martha, that's great that you have such a strong work ethic, but Mary is doing the right thing. She is doing what is needed." See, Mary chose to take time to be in Jesus' presence.

She knew she needed to take the opportunity to receive so she set everything else aside to be refreshed by His presence. Every person needs to take time to receive, to be refreshed and built up so we can live more effective lives. Sometimes we think we are doing a good thing by staying busy all the time, but if we are constantly "running on empty" not only are we cheating ourselves, we are cheating our families and the people around us because we aren't able to give them our best.

If you have ever flown in a commercial airplane, then you have heard the flight attendant's instructions informing passengers about airplane exits, emergency lighting, flotation devices, and oxygen masks that fall from above your head in case the cabin loses pressure. Then the flight attendant will say something like this: "Place the oxygen mask over your nose and mouth before assisting children or those around you." The truth is, we have to take care of ourselves first if we are going to take care of anyone else properly. We have to rejuvenate ourselves physically, spiritually, and emotionally if we arc going to live at our very best.

If you're like me, you make a to-do list every day: Run the kids to soccer; stop by the grocery store; finish a project at work. You rush here and there, taking care of all the things that matter most: the family, job, friends, church . . . *Oh yeah*, did you forget to put *yourself* on the list? Or do you need to move yourself up in priority on the list? Most of us try to take care of everyone else but ourselves, but we can't really give our best if we don't have our best to give. I heard someone say that you have to "show up" for yourself before you can "show up" for others. If you are constantly giving and never replenishing, you will be left feeling drained and frustrated. We are God's creation, and we have a responsibility to keep ourselves at our best. God never planned for us to live stressed-out and overbooked. He created the world and all that is in it, and then He took a day off. When is the last time you took the day off or took some time to recharge your batteries?

Today, find ways to invest in yourself physically, spiritually, and emotionally. Strengthen your spirit by spending time with the Father. Take care of your physical body by making healthy choices—maybe it's time to join a gym and get back in shape. Invest in yourself emotionally by doing the things you love. Even if it costs some money, remember you're worth it and the return will far outweigh the investment! You might be surprised at how a few small deposits in yourself can pay off in a big way. The important thing is that you take time to receive and enjoy it. If you had an expensive family heirloom, you would take care of it. You wouldn't mistreat it, let it get beat up or worn down, because it is valuable. Well, you are valuable, too, so make sure to take care of yourself!

Scripture Reading: Luke 10:38–42

 PRAYER FOR TODAY

Father God, today I choose to set my heart and mind on You. I come humbly into Your presence, because I know that You are the one thing that is needed. Fill me with Your grace; fill me with Your strength; fill me with Your joy; refresh me with Your truth. Teach me to take time to be still so that I can know You, my God. In Jesus' Name. Amen.

God's Most Amazing Work of Art

*"We are God's masterpiece. He has created us
anew in Christ Jesus, so we can do the good
things He planned for us long ago."*
Ephesians 2:10 (NLT)

You are God's own masterpiece! That means you are not ordinary or average; you are a one-of-a-kind original. When God created you, He went to great lengths to make you exactly the way He wanted you to be. You are His ultimate work of art.

Think, for a moment, about an artist creating a beautiful painting. That artist envisions what he is going to create and sees it in his mind long before he ever sees it on the canvas. As he paints, he carefully places each individual brushstroke with the understanding of how it fits in to the entire painting. There might be times when other people see his "work in progress" and they can't quite tell what it's going to be, but the artist always knows exactly what he is creating. And then, when his masterpiece is complete, the artist is so proud of his work! He admires his beautiful creation knowing that he has carefully poured himself into every detail. The artist loves it because he created it with his own hands, exactly the way he planned.

I want to remind you today that the greatest Artist of all time created you. He dreamed about you long before you were born, before a single brushstroke of your life took place. You may have days when you can't quite tell what He's creating on the canvas of your destiny. You may not always understand His "work in progress," but He knows what He's doing and He has your best interest in mind. He is pouring Himself into you, lovingly shaping every part of your life into an amazing masterpiece. It's time to see yourself as the valuable creation He lovingly designed.

I read a story one time about a man who lived in a tiny apartment and died in extreme poverty. At one point in his life, he had been homeless, living on the streets. This man never had any successes or notoriety to speak of; he lived and died as just another face in the crowd.

After the funeral, some family members went to his little run-down apartment to clear out his belongings. There was a painting that had been hanging on his wall for many years, which they decided to sell in a garage sale. A woman bought it and took it to a local art gallery for an appraisal. Much to her complete shock, the painting was extremely valuable. The piece of art that hung for so many years in that little run-down apartment was painted by a famous artist who lived in the early 1800s. The woman decided to auction off that painting and ended up selling it for several million dollars.

Just think how that poor man's life might have changed if he had known the value of what he possessed. He was a multimillionaire and didn't even know it. In the same way, so many people today are living with priceless treasure inside, and they aren't even aware of it. Sometimes, we have to appraise what's on the inside of us in order to really understand the value of who we are.

Today, don't settle for living a mediocre existence. See yourself the way God sees you. Every morning when you get out of bed, remind yourself, *I am a masterpiece. I am handpicked by God, and I am a person of extreme value and significance.* Remember, you are an original—you're not meant to be like everyone else; God designed you the way you are for a specific purpose. Everything about you is unique, and every detail about you matters. Receive His love today because His love isn't based on your performance; it's based on who He is. He never changes, and His love never changes. You belong to Him, and you are His most amazing work of art!

Scripture Reading: Ephesians 2:1–10

⌒⌒⌒ PRAYER FOR TODAY ⌒⌒⌒

Heavenly Father, thank You for creating me. Thank You for giving me vision and purpose and for pouring Your abundant life into me. Help me to see myself the way You see me, as a treasure with immeasurable value. I dedicate myself to You fresh and anew this day. May everything I do bring glory and honor to You. In Jesus' Name. Amen.

Actions Speak

Let your light shine before men,
that they may see your good deeds and
praise your Father in heaven.
Matthew 5:16 (NIV)

Everything we do produces a seed and leaves something for future generations. The Bible says, "Let your light shine before men, that they may see your good deeds" (Matthew 5:16 NIV). Notice, people may not necessarily *hear* your words, but they are certainly going to observe your life. For example, I can tell my children all day long how they are supposed to act and what they are supposed to do, but the truth is, they are going to do whatever they *see* me doing. When they grow up, they are going to model their lifestyles and their relationships after what they have experienced and observed. That is why it is so important to live as a positive example for your children and family. You paint a picture with your lifestyle, and your children put their own frame around it. Paint a picture that your children will be proud to frame, because your actions are building their future. And remember, it's never too late to change the picture you've been creating. You can create vision and purpose in your home that can be passed down for generations to come, because through your example you are investing not only in your own children but in your children's children too.

Maybe you don't have children of your own, but perhaps there are other children in your life. Tell your nieces, nephews, and your friends' children how important they are. Your words of faith in them will be a great deposit in their futures. Your actions speak, and you never know what can happen when you affect just one life.

In 1939, in a small East Texas town, a young man named Sam Martin would arrive at his high school early each morning and write scriptures on the chalkboard. He was passionate about sharing his faith even though the other students thought he was a little odd or "overboard" and they wouldn't have much to do with him. But one night, a fellow classmate was walking home from a nightclub at two o'clock in the morning. He began to think about eternity and what he was going to do with his life. This young man went home and randomly opened the family Bible. The page he turned to had a picture of Jesus standing at a door knocking. The caption read, "If anyone will open the door, I will come in."

The teenager's heart was stirred. He recalled the scriptures he had seen Sam write on the blackboard. The next day the young man asked Sam about the picture in his Bible and the scriptures he saw the night before. "Sam, why do you think I'm feeling this way?" he asked.

"That's God drawing you," Sam simply explained.

The next Sunday, Sam took his new friend to church. That day, John Osteen, Joel's father, made a decision for Christ and his life of faith began.

Sam went on to become a pastor, but he never spoke to large crowds of people like my father-in-law did. Sam didn't make an impact around the world like John Osteen. But that didn't matter. If it weren't for Sam Martin's positive influence, there may not have ever been a John Osteen or a Joel Osteen today. Fifty years later, Sam Martin wrote a book and titled it *I Touched One, but He Touched Millions*. That should be the title for each of our lives.

Remember, your life is significant. You are a part of God's eternal plan. You have a pivotal role to play in history. Don't ever underestimate the power of your actions. Be bold today and follow whatever God has placed in your heart. You may not be in the spotlight, but you will be rewarded for every good deed, for every person you encourage, for every act of kindness. When you touch one person, you are building a legacy of faith for future generations.

Scripture Reading: 2 Timothy 1:5–10

PRAYER FOR TODAY

Heavenly Father, thank You for making me a person of influence and for instilling Your purpose into my life. I desire to leave a legacy of faith and hope for future generations. Use me for Your glory, and show me ways that I can be a blessing to others and deposit good seeds for the future. In Jesus' Name. Amen.

Chapter Two

Living with Confidence

The Confidence Factor

God has not given us a spirit of fear
and timidity, but of power,
love, and self-discipline.
2 *Timothy 1:7 (NLT)*

Oftentimes, as soon as we make the decision to step out in faith and obey God, the Enemy comes at us with a load of fear to try to intimidate us and ultimately stop us. It starts with thoughts like, *What if you fail? What will other people think? You don't have what it takes.* If those seeds take root, they'll produce a harvest of weeds that will choke out your blessing. That's because fear is the enemy of confidence, designed to convince you to shrink back and settle for living an ineffective life.

The Bible says that fear is actually a spirit. It plays on our minds and emotions. It's been said that fear is an acronym for False Evidence Appearing Real. Fear is a lie, and the good news is that you have the truth of God's Word to combat it. It says in 1 John 4:18 that "perfect love casts out all fear." When you receive God's perfect love, it empowers you and deposits seeds of confidence in the soil of your heart. The only way to tap into those seeds and break the power of fear is to move forward. Confidence isn't built by playing it safe. It's not built when you simply stand still. It's built when you press past the fear that is trying to stop you.

Years ago, there was a television program called *Fear Factor*. Joel and I and our kids would pile up on the sofa after dinner to see the contestants attempt outrageous and daring stunts. We'd sit and watch in anticipation, wondering what the contestants would have to do next. Each stunt would test their ability to confront and overcome fear. If a contestant allowed fear to stop her, or even slow her down, she would be off the show and the camera would follow her down the dreaded "walk of shame." One person would be eliminated after each stunt until only the winner remained—the one who received the prize money.

Most of the time, the contestant who won not only overcame her fear but usually approached each task differently from the other contestants—with confidence. Confidence empowered the winner to perform the tasks faster, more skillfully, or with whatever proficiency was required. Many times we could tell who was going to win within the first few minutes just because we could see "the confidence factor" in the contestant's eyes.

That was only a television show, but how often does life play out this way? We have our goal in mind and set out to complete our mission, only to run straight into a wall of fear. Throughout life, we all have opportunities to either shrink back and settle where it's familiar, or we can take a step of faith and embrace the new things God has in store. Remember, you were never created to be stagnant. You were never created to take that "walk of shame"; you were created to win. Recognize that you have power over fear, and be determined to move forward past it. Let God's seeds of love produce a harvest of confidence inside of you!

Scripture Reading: Psalm 27

PRAYER FOR TODAY

Father in heaven, thank You for giving me power, love, and a self-disciplined spirit. I open my heart to You today and receive Your perfect love which drives fear out of my life. Fill me with Your confidence and assurance as I move forward in faith to embrace everything You have for me. In Jesus' Name. Amen.

Not "If," but "When"

What, then, shall we say in response to these
things? If God is for us, who can be against us?
Romans 8:31 (NIV)

It's amazing how empowering it is when someone has confidence in you. We all have times when we may not necessarily have confidence in ourselves, but, somehow, when the people around us believe in us, we can draw strength from it. That's why it's so important to surround yourself with the right people. When you position yourself in quality places with quality people, it will bring out your strengths and help you become the best possible version of yourself.

Most people are familiar with world-famous boxer Muhammad Ali and his renowned trainer, Angelo Dundee. But what many people don't know is that right before every boxing match Dundee would write down a number on a small slip of paper and place it inside Ali's glove. That may sound like a strange thing to do right before a boxer steps into the ring, but Dundee had a good reason for what he did. The number that he would write represented the round in which he predicted Ali would knock his opponent out. Dundee was so confident in Ali's ability that he didn't consider "if" Ali would win; he only considered "when"—and Ali knew it!

I love that story because it shows the confidence Ali's trainer had in him. Ali was well aware that Dundee knew what he was capable of, better than anyone else. I can imagine that Ali drew strength from Dundee's confidence and rose to the level of his expectations. I believe that level of confidence played a tremendous part in "the Champ's" amazing success as one of the greatest boxers that ever lived.

Do you know who has complete confidence in your ability to succeed? God does. Scripture says that He knew you before you were even born. He knows your abilities better than anyone else, and He believes in you! He knows what you're capable of and what's inside of you because He placed it in there. With God on your side, victory is imminent! You are more than a conqueror through Him! Even when you're not certain of the outcome, God is, and He has confidence in you. Let that sink down into your heart today—the God who holds the universe in the palm of His hand has faith in you! He's not wondering *if* you're going to win, He knows it's just a matter of time before you break through every barrier and overcome every obstacle. Victory is imminent!

When God created you, He deposited His seeds of success inside you. Have you ever stopped to think about how a seed works? A seed is actually dormant until it is placed in the right conditions. You can own seeds for every kind of tree, plant, and flower, but as long as they are in the packages, tucked away in a drawer somewhere, nothing will ever happen. Those seeds are full of tremendous potential just waiting for the right environment. At any time, you can take those same seeds and plant them in the right soil and give them the water and nutrients they need, and those very seeds that were once dormant will begin to grow and produce. The same is true for the seeds on the inside of you. Those seeds of greatness may have been lying dormant for a long time, but you are still full of tremendous potential. It's time to change your internal environment so those seeds can grow and produce the harvest for which they were intended.

The fact is, if Muhammad Ali *didn't* know that piece of paper was in his glove, it would have had no effect. In the same way, if you don't know what God has placed inside of you, it will have no effect. But when you start watering those seeds of greatness inside of you with the Word of God, they will begin to grow and flourish. It won't be long until you're overflowing with joy, peace, and confidence. You'll be able to knock out fear and boldly move forward into the victory He has prepared for you!

Scripture Reading: Romans 8:31–37

PRAYER FOR TODAY

Heavenly Father, thank You for the confidence that You have placed within me. Thank You for depositing seeds of greatness in my heart— seeds of hope, seeds of joy, seeds of victory. I set my heart and mind on Your Word, knowing that it is light and water to my soul. Today, I declare that I am more than conqueror, because You love me and are always with me. In Jesus' Name. Amen.

Give Your Faith a Voice

*Since we have the same spirit of faith, according
to what is written, "I believed and therefore I
spoke," we also believe and therefore speak.*
2 Corinthians 4:13 (NKJV)

Every believer has been given a measure of faith. In order to see
the promises of God come to pass in your life, you have to give
that faith a voice by declaring what God says in His Word.

The faith inside of you is activated by the words of your mouth.
Every word you speak is a seed that produces a harvest in your
future. That's why Scripture says, "Let the weak *say* I am strong."
When you give your faith a voice by declaring what God says about
you, the Bible says that He watches over His Word to bring it to
pass in your life. (See Jeremiah 1:12)

Now, one thing people do all the time is they speak the right
things and then turn around and "dig up" their good seed by speaking against it. They'll declare a promise and then start talking about
how bad everything is. "God is my Provider! . . . Look how bad the
economy is." But if we want to see our harvest of blessing, we can't
allow words of defeat or negativity to come out of our mouths. Instead, we have to water the good seeds by continuing to declare His
Word. When you wake up every morning, simply thank Him that

His promises are coming to pass in your life and keep an attitude of faith and expectancy.

This is what Joshua and Caleb did in the Old Testament. They declared what God was able to do, even when everyone else around them shrunk back in fear. Because of their faith, they were able to possess their Promised Land.

At the time, the children of Israel had just come out of Egypt, led by Moses, and they were on the verge of entering the land that God had promised. This Promised Land was already inhabited, so Moses sent twelve men—including Joshua and Caleb—to spy it out and report back to him. The inhabitants of the land were huge people—giants—strong and powerful. Certainly when the twelve Hebrew spies saw the giants, they were awestruck. I can imagine that over the many days they observed these giants, they saw things that invoked fear in their hearts. They may have seen the giants practicing their fighting skills or workers carrying huge boulders larger than what most humans could carry. Scripture doesn't really tell us what they saw, but apparently whatever it was, it terrified almost all the spies.

I would imagine that Joshua and Caleb were also impressed by what they saw. No doubt they, too, were tempted to fear the giants. But Joshua and Caleb had a different spirit than their companions. They understood what was inside of them, and they trusted God over what they saw with their eyes. While the other spies spoke out of their fear, saying to Moses, "We are but grasshoppers compared to the giants," Joshua and Caleb gave their faith a voice and declared, "We are well able to overcome! Let us go at once and possess the land." Because Joshua and Caleb stood strong in their position of faith, they were able to push past fear and move forward into their destiny. And out of that entire generation, they were the only two who ever made it into the Promised Land.

We all have giants or obstacles that try to keep us from possessing what God has promised. We have two choices: we can quit and live in mediocrity, or we can fight and take hold of the victory. Today, don't let your circumstances dictate what's coming out of your mouth; instead, let what comes out of your mouth dictate your circumstances. As you give your faith a voice, no matter what anyone else is saying around you, God will bless you and promote you, and it won't be long until you are entering your Promised Land!

Scripture Reading: Numbers 13:26–31

PRAYER FOR TODAY

Father in heaven, today I declare that with You on my side, I am well able to conquer in this life. I choose to believe Your Word above my circumstances, above my feelings, and above the voices around me or mistakes from the past. I know that You have promised me victory, and so today I rise up in faith and boldly move forward to possess every promise You have for me. In Jesus' Name. Amen.

Step Over the Line

Whether you turn to the right or to the left,
your ears will hear a voice behind you,
saying, "This is the way; walk in it."
Isaiah 30:21 (NIV)

W hen you are following God's plan for your life, it is certain that you will find yourself in uncharted territory. Sometimes lack of experience and feelings of inadequacy hold us back. We long to do something fresh and exciting, but as we gaze into the unknown, we find it difficult to take that first step because we just aren't sure if we are "enough."

Perhaps you have an opportunity before you that seems intimidating. Maybe you want to start a new career, but you are afraid that you won't be able to succeed. Or your lack of experience as a homeowner has stopped you from buying your first home. While it may be true that you lack experience, let me assure you that God does not, and when you rely on Him, He will equip you to excel at whatever you set your hand to.

I can remember the feelings of inadequacy I had to overcome when Joel and I took over as pastors of Lakewood Church. I didn't have much experience in public speaking, and I dreaded getting up each Sunday and speaking in front of thousands of people. I would find myself uptight all week long. My mind was racing, full of anxiety and thoughts of doubt and defeat. It was as if there was a line of fear right in front of me that was trying to force me to quit. One day I finally realized what was happening. The dread that I felt was just a symptom of fear that was trying to paralyze me. It was threatening to keep me from stepping into a new experience and growing to the next level.

Joel would encourage me repeatedly, "Victoria, we are in this together. If we are going to take this ministry to the next level, we both need to do our part." Even though I recognized it was fear trying to stop me, that didn't make it any easier. The fear didn't go away just because I recognized it; I had to recognize something else: that God had planted seeds inside of me to enable me to do whatever I needed to do. His grace was upon me, empowering me to fulfill my calling. I had a choice to make: either allow those seeds to spring forth and give me the confidence I needed, or allow them to remain dormant and surrender to the fear that was paralyzing me. I made the decision that I was not going to allow fear to hold me back.

The next time I had to step out on that platform, I envisioned myself bigger than that fear. I kept telling myself that I am strong, talented, and well able. I took captive every negative thought and made it obedient to the Word of God. I also envisioned God waiting right there for me with open arms, giving me the strength and confidence to take that next step. As I did this, I could feel my confidence growing and I saw myself moving forward, stepping over the line of fear, into His loving arms.

From then on, every time I approached the platform, I visualized that scene until my fear was replaced with confidence. I felt like those seeds inside me had blossomed into full-fledged oak trees! Now each time I step onto the platform to speak, I tell myself, *God chose me, He has equipped me, and I am able to do what He says I can do.*

Always remember, victory starts in your mind. When you meditate on the truth that God is for you and He has a good plan for you, those seeds of faith will spring forth, and you will see yourself as He sees you, capable of doing whatever He has called you to do. Today, choose to step over the line of fear into the life of blessing He has for you!

Scripture Reading: Psalm 23:1–6

 PRAYER FOR TODAY

Dear God, today I come to You with an open heart, ready to receive Your grace and strength. Help me to see myself the way You see me: strong, talented, and well able. I choose to take captive every negative thought and make it obedient to Your Word as I step over the line of fear. Thank You for the work You are doing in me. In Jesus' Name. Amen.

Swing Just One More Time

The godly may trip seven times, but they will get up again.
Proverbs 24:16 (NLT)

George Herman "Babe" Ruth Jr. is known as perhaps the greatest baseball player of all time. He hit 714 home runs in his career, and for almost four decades, he held the major league lifetime home-run record. Legend has it that during the 1932 World Series, he actually pointed to a spot on the outfield wall and then hit a home run directly over that spot. He was known as "The Babe," "The Bambino," and "The Sultan of Swat." In fact, Yankee Stadium is still known today as "The House That Ruth Built." He was a legend even during his own lifetime.

But what many people don't know about Babe Ruth is that before he ever held the record for the most home runs, he held the record for being struck out! That's right—the Great Bambino knew well the walk back to the dugout, which means you can add "Strikeout King" to his list of titles. In fact, Ruth struck out 1,330 times—more than any other player in his era.

You would have thought that at some point during his reign as the "Strikeout King," he would have been embarrassed or a bit discouraged. I doubt if anyone would have blamed him if he had decided to just sit the next game out. But he didn't. You might have also thought that since he was constantly striking out, he would have started doing things a bit differently. Perhaps he would have changed his batting stance or decided not to swing so hard, but he didn't. You see, way before Babe Ruth became the lifetime home-run leader, he saw himself as successful. Even when it looked like nothing was further from the truth, even when his circumstances screamed "failure," the Babe refused to allow his past mistakes to affect his future. Instead, he saw himself on a mission—to hit more home runs than anyone else. He was not going to allow the fear of failure to get in the way of his destiny. He knew those home runs were inside of him, just one swing away.

So I ask you today: What do you do when you "strike out" in life? Do you just give up and put your bat away, or do you stand strong, knowing that you're one swing closer to that home run? Holding on to past mistakes amplifies the fear of failure, which in turn robs so many people of their confidence, causing them to sit in the dugout of life. But just like the Babe, you have to realize that there are seeds of greatness inside of you just waiting to burst forth. Don't let your past mistakes or failures steal your God-given destiny. Today, you are also on a mission, and no matter where you've left your bat, you can pick it up, get back in the game, and keep on swinging, because now is the time for you to knock that ball right out of the park and possess the victory God has in store for you!

Scripture Reading: Psalm 37:23–31

∽ PRAYER FOR TODAY ∽

Heavenly Father, thank You for empowering me to succeed in every area of my life. Today, I choose to shake off past failures, old mind-sets, wrong thinking, and anything that would hold me back. I choose to "swing" again, knowing that I am one step closer to the victory You have prepared for me. In Jesus' Name. Amen.

Reaching New Levels

*The path of the righteous is like the morning sun,
shining ever brighter till the full light of day.*
Proverbs 4:18 (NIV)

God wants us to constantly be rising to new levels and reaching new heights in this life. He wants us to grow and flourish and excel at whatever we set our hand to. But so many people stay right where they are, settling for less than God's best because they've grown accustomed to their circumstances and they are comfortable. But if we are going to experience all that God has for us, we can't just stay where we are; we have to stretch and step out of our comfort zones.

Reaching new levels isn't always easy—but it wasn't meant to be easy. If everything were easy all the time, you wouldn't stretch. You wouldn't stretch your faith, you wouldn't increase, and you would miss out on discovering so many facets of God's character. Every time we step out, we learn more about who God is and what He's deposited on the inside of us. Every time you take a step of faith, every time you stretch, you are tapping into all that He has placed on the inside of you.

Stretching is good for you. It's good for your body and it's good for your mind. Stretching builds your confidence. Your life of faith begins by God doing a work *in* you, and then you begin to work *with* Him. The more new situations you experience, the more you will stretch, and the more confidence you will have. Sometimes stretching is uncomfortable, but it prepares you for the challenges that line the road to your destiny.

Oftentimes God will use other people in our lives to stretch us and help us out of our comfort zones. I can remember when I was about thirteen years old, my mother began taking me to work with her in the jewelry store she owned. I didn't like to go, but my mother knew that getting me out of my comfort zone would help me stretch and grow. She was so proud to have me with her, but to me it was pure torture! Here I was, a young girl expected to sell expensive jewelry to adults. I was intimidated by the whole experience. I would rather have gone to the dentist than wait on customers! I didn't think I was qualified and doubt often filled my mind. There was so much to know about diamonds, rubies, and sapphires that I certainly didn't know. What if a customer asked me to design a ring or a necklace? I didn't know how to do that. I was certain that there were at least one hundred ways to embarrass myself. I was out of my comfort zone and I didn't like it. Sometimes I would actually hide in the back of the store until all the other sales people were busy with customers and I had no choice but to go out onto the sales floor.

My mother understood my fears and insecurities as well as my gifts and talents. She knew that I had everything inside me to succeed, but she also knew that I wasn't going to reach my full potential sitting at home on the couch. She began teaching me and mentoring me. First, she just asked me to stand next to her while she helped customers. Then, each day she would instruct me on the origins and attributes of a particular gemstone. Gradually, she began teaching me how to design jewelry. As I matured in the business, she would ask my opinion and often take my advice. She would congratulate me on a successful sale and give me pointers when I failed. She would tell me how much the customers liked me and how they would ask for me when I was not there.

Eventually, I learned to love jewelry design and became knowledgeable in the trade. In time, I became skillful both in selling and in buying jewelry for the business. God used my mother to help me discover my inner strengths. By stretching me one step at a time, He was allowing me to see that I could succeed even in unfamiliar territory, and you can too! You never know what God has for you right around the corner when you step out of your comfort zone. In fact, years later, it was in that same jewelry store that I dreaded so much as a teenager where I met Joel. He came in for a watch battery one afternoon, and I sold him a brand new watch. He loves to tease and say that I've been taking his money ever since! But if I would have stayed in my comfort zone as a teenager, I might have missed meeting the man of my dreams. Looks like Mother knows best after all!

I encourage you today to stay open to what God wants to do in your life. If you will allow Him to, He will stretch you, one step at a time. He will put people in your path who recognize your talents and are willing to help you discover your inner strengths. Be willing to step out of that comfort zone because there are new levels of greatness in store for you!

Scripture Reading: Philippians 2:12-18

⌒⌒⌒ PRAYER FOR TODAY ⌒⌒⌒

Heavenly Father, thank You for working in my life. Thank You for growing and stretching me, for molding me into Your image. I choose today to press past the familiar, to take a step of faith forward, knowing that You are with me. Thank You for increasing me and making me more effective for Your glory. In Jesus' Name. Amen.

Tending to the Vision

He who tends a fig tree will eat its fruit.
Proverbs 27:18 (NIV)

Many people today have the mentality that says: "the grass is greener on the other side." They look at others who appear to be more successful and think, *Boy, they must be lucky.* And then they look at their own circumstances and think, *If only . . . If only I had a better job. If only my spouse were like so-and-so. If only I had gone to college. If only I had the opportunities so-and-so had.* It's easy for people to look around and think everyone else has it better than they do. But I believe this kind of comparison will get you off course and keep you from God's best. If we assume that other people just happen to have it better, it gives us an excuse to live in mediocrity. The truth is, the principles of God's Word apply to every person. We all have the same opportunity to receive blessing, peace, joy, and victory if we are willing to tend to the vision that's inside of us.

I don't personally believe the grass is greener on the other side; I believe the grass is greener where you water it. In other words, we have to tend to the things that are inside of us if we want to see our lives blossom and grow. If you want better relationships, you have to invest in the people around you. If you want a better job, you have to invest in your skill set to qualify for that promotion and then go after it. We all have the capacity to come up higher. God has given *you* tremendous opportunities, and that's why you can't focus on what everyone else has. If you do, you'll miss out on what God has especially for you! It doesn't matter where you've come from; it doesn't matter where you are starting from now. If you'll just step out and be faithful with what is in your hand today, God will bless it and multiply it and take you places that you never dreamed.

There's a story about a woman who was newly divorced, almost penniless, afraid of public places, and trying to raise two teenage sons. Through several tragedies in her life, she developed severe agoraphobia, a fear of leaving her house. She searched her heart for ways to support herself and her two sons.

She loved to cook, and all she knew to do for income was to make sandwiches and other simple foods to sell to people in the area. She found a few customers, but because she was so uncomfortable leaving the house, her two sons had to deliver the sandwiches. As she sat in her house, she could imagine her business growing, and she began to see success in her future. Her business quickly grew beyond the size of her kitchen, and that's when the real work began. Even though she was afraid, even though she was uncomfortable, she knew she had a choice to make: to shrink back and stay in her comfort zone or to keep tending to the vision that was inside of her so it could grow. She made a decision to stretch herself— one step at a time. First, she decided to confront the agoraphobia that imprisoned her. Reaching deep inside herself, she was able to take a job as a chef at a local hotel. Once again she experienced tremendous success. A few years later, she opened her own restaurant, The Lady and Sons, right in the heart of Savannah, Georgia. The restaurant's reputation quickly spread and received national recognition. Paula Deen's restaurant was such a success that she eventually landed her own television show, published cookbooks, and even had a role on the silver screen. Today she is one of America's most beloved television chefs, and it was because she was willing to do whatever it took to tend to the vision that was inside of her.

Today, instead of focusing on what you don't have, look inside at what you do have. Make the decision to cultivate the dry, fallow areas of your life. Begin to water and invest in the areas where you want to see change. Get a vision and dedicate it to the Lord. As you tend to what the Lord has given you, I believe He'll pour out His blessing and favor and you'll see your life flourish beyond anything you could have ever hoped or dreamed.

Scripture Reading: Matthew 25:14–28

 PRAYER FOR TODAY

Father in heaven, thank You for the opportunities You have prepared for me. Today, I renounce comparison and choose to focus on the gifts and talents You have placed inside of me. I look forward to the future with great expectation, knowing that You are ordering my steps. In Jesus' Name. Amen.

Pull Back the Curtain of Fear

The LORD is good, a stronghold in the day of trouble;
and He knows those who trust in Him.
Nahum 1:7 (NKJV)

What an amazing thought: God knows the people who trust in Him. If we look at the word "know," one definition is *to recognize the nature of something*. When you put your trust in God, God recognizes and identifies with your nature, because it is part of His nature. He is drawn to trust. Trust gives Him something to work with and opens the door for Him to move in your life.

I talk to people all the time who have a difficult time trusting God because they are overwhelmed with fear, doubt, and insecurity. Those things are the opposite of God's nature. He doesn't operate in the realm of fear; He can't identify with fear because He doesn't *know* fear. If we are really going to know the Father and trust Him with every area of our lives, we have to pull back the curtain of fear that stands in the way.

Do you know that fear isn't reality? It's only a thought in your mind. It's like in that classic movie *The Wizard of Oz*: When Dorothy arrived at the Emerald City, the great Wizard of Oz appeared to be all-powerful and mysterious, and he made everyone tremble. He seemed larger than life.

That's what fear does to us—it presents itself as larger than life, intimidates us, and makes us tremble. Fear can seem overwhelming and all-powerful. But when Dorothy and her friends pulled back the curtain, they discovered that the "wizard" was just an ordinary man, blowing smoke, and pushing a lot of buttons. In the same way, one of the most important things you can do in your life is to learn to pull back the curtain of fear so you can see it for what it really is—*the Enemy blowing a lot of smoke and pushing your buttons!*

Fear has no power over you unless you give it power by focusing on it, dwelling on it, talking about it, and doing nothing about it. However, when you turn your focus to God, when you dwell on His Word, when you press past fear and declare your trust in Him, not only are you starving fear, but you are feeding your faith and empowering yourself through the Word of God.

Today, I encourage you to search your heart and mind and see if there's a curtain of fear or doubt deceiving you in any area. Make the decision to pull back the curtain and expose that fear for the lie that it really is. Then begin speaking God's Word to erase the lie and replace it with the truth. For example, if you have a curtain of fear in the area of your finances, begin declaring Philippians 4:19: "My God shall supply all my needs according to His riches in glory." If you have a curtain of fear regarding something in your future, declare Jeremiah 29:11: "God has good plans for my future, plans to prosper me and not to harm me." Get to know His Word and make it your number one priority, because when you know His Word, you know Him. And when you know Him, you trust Him. Don't let a curtain of fear come between you and God any longer. He is good and He loves you with an everlasting love. Press past fear and render it powerless by putting your trust in Him!

Scripture Reading: Proverbs 3:1–10

⌒⌒⌒⌒ PRAYER FOR TODAY ⌒⌒⌒⌒

Heavenly Father, today I receive Your Word, which is truth and life to my soul. I choose to pull back the curtain of fear so I can see the good plans You have for me. Give me Your wisdom and discernment. Fill me with Your grace and peace. Thank You for directing my steps into the good future You have prepared for me. In Jesus' Name. Amen.

Chapter Three

Embracing
What's Important

What Is in Your Hand?

The LORD said to [Moses], "What is that in your hand?"
Exodus 4:2 (NIV)

Have you ever started to pursue a dream in your heart and then become overwhelmed by it, wondering if you were equipped or qualified to pull it off? If you have, you're certainly not the first one. In fact, many of the great men and women of the Bible struggled with the same issue. For example, so often when we think of Moses, we remember him as the great spiritual giant who led the Israelites out of captivity, but did you know that Moses doubted himself? He didn't feel equipped all the time. In fact, he was self-conscious because he had a stuttering problem. But God simply said to him, "What do you have in your hand?" In the next few moments, God showed Moses that it didn't matter what he thought he needed; the God of the universe had already equipped him with everything he needed to accomplish his destiny.

Today, the same is true for you. God will place in your hand whatever you need in order to fulfill your purpose in this life. However, many people have the tendency to hold on to things that God never intended for them to hold on to, and when your hands are full of other things, it's difficult to take hold of what God has for you. People fill their hands with lots of good things; they take on noteworthy obligations and fill their arms with impressive accomplishments. But "good" can be the enemy of "best." We have to constantly evaluate what we have in our hands and be willing to let go of some things in order to embrace the best that God has for us.

One day I was in the kitchen at Lakewood Church, making some hot tea. Several other people were taking a break, too, and the place was buzzing with activity. I had my tea in one hand and a spoon in the other, and I was just about to stir, when suddenly I looked up to see my little five-year-old nephew, Christopher, pushing through the crowd and running straight for me. Now, Christopher was less than half my size, but he is all boy, strong and solid, and on top of that, he doesn't recognize his own strength. I knew I had to brace myself for what was about to happen. A split second later, Christopher plowed right into me, grabbing me around the legs and squeezing me as tightly as he could! With all the energy he could muster, Christopher was loving me, and with all that I could muster, I was trying not to spill my hot tea! As much as I wanted to embrace Christopher, my hands were full, so at that moment, I couldn't. I had to put down what I had in my hands first in order to wrap my arms around little Christopher and return his embrace. Not only was I able to enjoy Christopher's love, but I was able to give love back to him. There was an exchange that took place when I let go of what was in my hands.

How often do we go through life holding on to things we think are important but are not? Is there something you are holding on to today, something you know you need to let go of to make room for what God is trying to do in your life? Is your schedule overloaded? Are you clinging to a relationship that you know is destructive? Are your thoughts consumed with a situation from your past? You might even be holding on to something good, but good things can also keep our hands too full to embrace God's very best. That day in the kitchen, I was simply holding a cup of tea. It was neither good nor bad, but it was keeping me from something better.

Today, I encourage you to evaluate what you have in your hands. Be willing to let go of anything that is keeping you from God's best.

Make room for what He has for you, knowing that He is ready to bless you and equip you to fulfill the destiny He has placed in your heart.

Scripture Reading: Exodus 4:1–14

PRAYER FOR TODAY

Heavenly Father, today I open my hands and my heart to You. Give me wisdom to discern what I should hold on to and what I should release. I trust that You will place in my hands everything I need to be successful in this life. Thank You for using me for Your glory. In Jesus' Name. Amen.

Take Off the Limits

O LORD, how many are my foes!
How many rise up against me! . . . but you
are a shield around me, O LORD; you bestow
glory on me and lift up my head.
Psalm 3:1–3 (NIV)

So many people today feel stuck in their circumstances. They live narrow, limited lives, thinking things like, *That's it. That's all there is. There aren't any other options for me.* They limit themselves to what they can see or what they knew growing up. If no one else in their families went to college, they think they can't either. They let other people define their limits, or they allow their resources or circumstances to define their limits. If that's you today, realize that you are not limited by your circumstances: your past, the economy, or what you have been told you can or can't do. You are the only one who sets the limits for your life, and today you can take the limits off.

When King David wrote today's scripture in Psalm 3, he was in a very difficult situation. He was actually running for his life from his very own son who wanted to kill him and take over the throne. Can you imagine?! David was probably feeling overwhelmed, distraught, heartbroken, betrayed, and abandoned. Do any of those feelings sound familiar? But notice that David didn't just tell the Lord all about his problems. He didn't just sit and think, *Looks like it's all over for me. I guess there's no way out.* No. David declared his faith when he said, "*But* you, God, are a shield around me" (italics added). David made the choice to take his eyes off his circumstances and set his gaze on what God could do in his life. He was willing to stay open, and when his circumstances didn't give him any options, he knew there was an option he couldn't see. He chose to broaden his thinking to include the unseen supernatural realm. When he did, he took off all the limits, and God miraculously delivered him.

Limits are set in your mind. There will always be difficult situations. There will always be opposition. There will always be critics and naysayers in life. It's not what they say about you that matters, but what you say and believe about yourself and your God. Don't allow your circumstances or the opinions of others to cause you to water down your dreams. You were not created to settle for mediocrity. One of the most important things you can learn is that other people don't have to believe in you in order for your dreams to come to pass. God believes in you; therefore you can believe in yourself.

Today, no matter how things look around you, remember you are not limited! Follow David's example, and instead of just telling God about what's happening in the natural, take the limits off by declaring His Word over your life. Circumstances may be tough, but you are not limited, *because God* is working behind the scenes on your behalf. You may have a difficult relationship, but you are not limited, *because God* is your Restorer. You may have an overwhelming need, but you are not limited, *because God* is your Provider! The doctors may have told you that you have an incurable disease, but you are not limited, *because God* is your Healer! Things may look impossible today, but you are not limited, *because with God*, all things are possible! Keep that constant attitude of faith and victory, and make room for the limitless God to move mightily on your behalf!

Scripture Reading: Psalm 3:1–8

PRAYER FOR TODAY

Father God, thank You for always being faithful and for working in my life, even when I can't see it. Today I open my heart to You, knowing that when I feel limited, You are not limited. I open my mind to You and choose to remove the limits. I know that with You, all things are possible! In Jesus' Name. Amen.

The God Option

I am making a way in the wilderness
and streams in the wasteland.
Isaiah 43:19b (NIV)

Many times in our lives, Joel and I had to be open to what we couldn't see and didn't understand in order to make room for what was in our future. This was especially true when Joel's father passed away. At first we couldn't see how the details could work out, and it seemed that our options were limited.

Up until that point, Joel had invested more than seventeen years of his life working with his father behind the scenes in the television ministry. Not only did they work closely together, they were great friends, and Joel's entire career was tied to his father's ministry. His father was the one ministering out front, while Joel was working behind the scenes, building and expanding the television ministry. That was what he was trained to do, and that's what he enjoyed doing. But when his father died suddenly, Joel had to be flexible and open to a new way of thinking about the direction of his life. He had to let go of any preconceived ideas he had about himself to make room for what God wanted to do next in his life. It wasn't easy, but Joel had to reposition his thinking and let go of the mind-set that he was just a behind-the-scenes person. Although it didn't look as if there were many good options, when Joel let go and allowed God to reshape his thinking, he was able to get a vision for the future and see the *God option*. He embraced the change and believed that God was using it to take us to the next level. Even though it was difficult, we realized that Joel's dad had run his race and had passed the baton to us. This was the time to rise up, not sit down. Our determination to be open and to make room for whatever God wanted to do was the key that opened the door of God's blessing in our lives, launching us into the ministry we are in today.

God has placed in you everything you need to rise higher, too, but you can't set your focus on what you see in the natural, you have to keep yourself open to your *God option*. You have to be willing to embrace change and keep the right perspective even when that change is unexpected. You can't automatically assume the worst because God is always working to bring forth good out of your difficulties.

Have you experienced a loss in your life? Do you need to reposition yourself today? Whether it was the loss of a loved one or the loss of a job or even the loss of a dream, God still has a good plan for your life. Stay open and be willing to change. Whenever a door in your life closes, God always gives you the grace to move forward. He is a progressive God, and He always wants us to rise higher; He wants us to let go of anything that would try to hold us captive. Don't get stuck thinking that there aren't any good options. There's always the *God option*. Remember, your life has seasons; there is a season to mourn a loss, but there is also a season to press on to the new things God wants you to do. It's so important to reach a point where you are ready to let go of yesterday and embrace the future God has for you.

I encourage you today—be willing to look beyond where you are right now, and be open to what *God* can do in your life. You may not see any other options now, but remember, you always have the *God option*.

Scripture Reading: Exodus 15:1–6

PRAYER FOR TODAY

Father God, today I choose to take my eyes off my circumstances and focus on You. I trust that You are good and that You are working behind the scenes on my behalf. Even when it looks like I don't have any options, God, I know that You can make a way where there seems to be no way. I choose to keep myself open to what You have in store for me—my God option! In Jesus' Name. Amen.

He Orders Your Steps

We can make our plans, but the LORD determines our steps.
Proverbs 16:9 (NLT)

In Genesis 12, God tells Abraham to leave his homeland and go to a new place. It didn't make a lot of sense to Abraham, because he was comfortable where he was. He had family and friends, and he was familiar with the land. Abraham could have easily chosen to stay right where he was, but he knew that if he would let go of the familiar, God would give him something better.

Abraham and his family, along with his nephew Lot and Lot's entire family, packed up their belongings and their herds and headed out into the unknown. As time went on, they experienced so much increase in their livestock that the land couldn't support both families, so Lot and Abraham agreed to part ways. Abraham offered Lot the opportunity to choose which land he wanted to settle on. He said to Lot, "Which direction do you want to go? You choose first, and I'll take whatever is left." Lot looked out as far as he could see in both directions and chose the best part of the land, the plain of Jordan. Scripture describes it as a well-watered garden, so beautiful and lush. I imagine it may have looked like Hawaii, even though it was in the Middle East. When Abraham saw what was in the other direction, it didn't look like Hawaii; it looked more like the desert.

It didn't look very appealing—there were few trees and little grass. It would have been easy for Abraham to think, *Man, I got the short end of this deal. God, where is the favor You showed me in the past? I'm the one who had the assignment. Why is this happening? If only I would have chosen first!*

Have you ever felt that way? Have you found yourself thinking, *God, I'm doing everything right. I'm following your voice, I'm obeying your commands, and I'm showing kindness to people, yet I'm the one missing out.* Oftentimes, the very thing you think is working against you is really going to work out for you. However, it's up to you to release preconceived ideas, let go of thinking everything has to happen your way and on your timetable, and trust that God is ordering your steps.

If you have been going through some changes in your life that you don't understand, or if it looks like you don't have the favor you once had in a certain area, God may be stirring you out of the old so He can bring you into something new and better. It's not always comfortable, and it may not always be the easiest way. Sometimes it may look like you missed out, but if you will embrace the future before you and keep an attitude of faith and expectancy, then God can open the right doors so you can get to where you need to be.

When Lot chose the best part of the land, Abraham never complained or criticized him. He didn't try to bargain with him for half of that land. He didn't question God; he just trusted. Right after all this took place, the Lord said to Abraham, "Lift up your eyes from where you are and look north and south, east and west. All the land that you see I will give to you and your offspring forever" (Genesis 13:14–15 NIV). What an amazing promise! God honored Abraham, and later, when God told Abraham that Sarah would give birth to the first offspring, it says that Abraham believed God and it was accounted to him as righteousness (see Genesis 15:6). I can imagine that Abraham looked out over the barren land that was soon to be his home and thought, *This is going to be exciting to see how God turns this around.*

I am personally amazed at how Abraham let go of something

good in anticipation of something better. And, of course, God fulfilled His promise to Abraham, and He will fulfill His promise to you! Today, trust that He is ordering your steps even when it looks like you are getting the short end of the deal. Remember He is faithful and He is leading you into a place of blessing and increase.

Scripture Reading: Genesis 12

PRAYER FOR TODAY

Heavenly Father, thank You for another day to praise You, another day to see Your miracle-working power in my life. Even when I don't see how things are going to work out, I trust that You have a plan. I know that Your ways are higher than mine. Today, I rest in You and look forward to the good things You have for me. In Jesus' Name. Amen.

Avoid the Traps

*Whoever tries to keep his life will lose it, and
whoever loses his life will preserve it.*
Luke 17:32–33 (NIV)

Have you ever heard how hunters used to trap monkeys? The hunters would fill a large barrel with bananas and then cut a small hole in the side of it, just barely big enough for the monkey to get his hand and arm through. The monkey, completely unaware of the trap, would reach his arm into the barrel and grab one of those bananas. But when he tried to pull his arm out, he couldn't get his clenched fist and the banana back out of the hole. The monkey wanted that banana so badly that he wouldn't release it. Consequently, the hunters would easily capture the monkey. It's interesting that at any point prior to the capture, the monkey could have simply let go of the banana and pulled his hand out of the barrel, but he was so focused on what he wanted that he didn't even realize he was in a trap!

Many people live like that today—with both hands clenched, so focused on trying to hold on to what they have that they don't realize it is robbing them of the freedom and victory God has in store. Don't let that be you! Choose to release anything that's keeping you from God's best because nothing in this world is worth holding on to so tightly. Don't get trapped because you aren't willing to change or reposition yourself or your thinking. Remember, God always has your best in mind. His plans are for your good, and when you follow His plans, you can move forward in peace, strength, joy, faith, and victory.

Remember, the best way to avoid the traps is to choose to live a life of faith. Scripture tells us that faith comes by hearing the Word of God. Developing your faith is a process, and God leads us one step at a time. Be open and let Him lead you and reposition you. Don't let fear trap you or hold you back. Be bold and keep moving forward. You already have everything you need to be successful in your future. If you need strength, it's on the inside of you. If you need hope, it's on the inside of you. If you need joy, determination, or encouragement, God has placed it within you. Tap into your God-given resources by faith, and trust Him, because He will never ask you to do something that He hasn't already prepared you to do. Today, set yourself up for freedom and victory by being open-handed and open-minded to what God wants to do in your life.

Scripture Reading: Matthew 6:19–24

PRAYER FOR TODAY

Heavenly Father, I come into Your presence today with thanksgiving and praise because You are good. Search me and know my heart. Remove anything that would keep me from Your very best. Give me wisdom and discernment to avoid the traps of the world, and help me to stay on the good path You have prepared for my life. In Jesus' Name. Amen.

Move Past "If Only"

*I focus on this one thing: Forgetting the past
and looking forward to what lies ahead.*
Philippians 3:13 (NLT)

When things don't go as planned, most people automatically try to figure out why. It's good to evaluate yourself and look for ways to do better next time, but you have to be careful not to start overanalyzing, because that can get you stuck. If you're always looking where to place the blame, or if you're getting swallowed up in the "whys," then you're headed in the wrong direction. It doesn't take long to slip into the "if only" syndrome . . . *If only I had gone to college,* or, *If only I had married that person,"* or, *"If only I had qualified for that new home."* But realize today that you can't move forward if you're living your life looking backward. You can't change the past, so why not look forward to where God is taking you? It may look as though you missed something good, but remember, God always has something better in store.

Years ago when Joel and I were first married, we decided to buy a home. We found one that looked perfect for us: it was located in a neighborhood with other young families, it was on a beautiful lot, and it had a swimming pool—something I always wanted.

We made the best offer we could on the property and prayed and believed that the owners would accept it. Day after day went by, but we didn't hear anything. We kept speaking words of faith, declaring, "This is our house!" No one was living in it at the time, so we would go over to it in the evening and sit outside, study it, and dream about it. But unfortunately the homeowners didn't accept our offer. The door totally closed, and I was so disappointed. I thought for sure that was the house we were supposed to have. I found myself tempted to say *if only* we had offered more. *If only* we had prayed harder. *If only* we had acted sooner, on and on. But instead of mourning over what didn't work out, I made the choice to let it go and believe that God had something better in store.

Right after we heard the news about the house, I found another property that caught my attention. It was an old, run-down house on a beautiful lot in a valuable neighborhood. It was actually abandoned with broken windows, no landscaping, and a scarecrow in the kitchen to keep the animals out! It didn't look like much, but down deep I believed it was right for us. We put in a bid on that house, and sure enough, our offer was accepted.

Truthfully, I wasn't as excited about this house as I was the first one. It didn't have a swimming pool like I dreamed of; instead it had crooked floors! The foundation was cracked, and some of the interior doors wouldn't close. I had to put blocks under my sofa just to keep it from leaning forward. Friends and family used to make jokes about those crooked floors, but I grew to love that house. I knew God gave us that house, so I wasn't going to look back and focus on what I didn't get. That house didn't look like the "perfect" house, but it was the right place for that season.

We lived in that house for three years, and God blessed us beyond our wildest dreams. We ended up dividing our lot and selling half of it for the same price we originally paid for the entire piece of property! We were able to build a new home for less than what we would have paid for the first house we wanted. God used that crooked-floored house to bring us through a journey of faith. That's where we learned to trust Him and believe that He always knows what's best, even when we weren't getting what we thought we wanted. Even though, in the natural, it looked like we were going backward, that time actually helped us move forward spiritually. Our experience with that house gave us courage to trust God in a new way and equipped us for years down the road when we would take a basketball arena and turn it into a magnificent house of worship!

Today, I'm not living in a house with crooked floors. I'm living in a house more beautiful than I ever dreamed we would own, but I'm convinced that if I would have been unhappy over what didn't work out, my attitude would have kept me from God's best. Today, if you're thinking, *Life would have been different if only I had this or if only that had happened*, let it go. Trust that God is guiding your steps. It may not make a lot of sense right now, but if you'll let go of those things that didn't work out and stay in faith, He will take you to exactly where you need to be.

Scripture Reading: Proverbs 3:21–26

 PRAYER FOR TODAY

Heavenly Father, I love You and bless You today. Thank You for the work You are doing in my life. I choose to trust You even when things don't make sense, even when things don't work out the way I planned. I know that You are good and that You have good things in store for my future. I trust You with my whole heart. In Jesus' Name. Amen.

Choosing Right Relationships

There is a time for everything, and a season
for every activity under heaven: . . . a time
to embrace and a time to refrain.
Ecclesiastes 3:1, 5 (NIV)

One of the most important decisions you can make on the road to your destiny is choosing who you will allow into your life, who you will spend your time with and ultimately partner with on your life's journey. If you are going to love your life, you have to be in the right relationships, and when you recognize that a relationship is unhealthy, you have to be willing to let go so you can be free to receive what God has for you.

Are there influences in your life that you know are not right? Are you spending too much time with friends who are putting your destiny at jeopardy? Is there a commitment you are about to make in a relationship you're unsure of? If you are seeing red flags but you're afraid to let go because you don't want to be alone, remember God will never leave you alone; you are too important to Him.

My friend Shannon grew up with a heart for God, but as a young woman in her mid twenties, her life became focused on other things, namely her career as a journalist that was taking off. It appeared from the outside that she had a storybook life—complete with her Prince Charming boyfriend. Their reality, however, was that they had a tumultuous relationship. But Shannon had grown accustomed to the ups and downs and believed that any relationship was better than no relationship at all. Besides that, she thought she could change him, so she convinced herself to stay with the "prince."

Despite how comfortable the relationship had become, Shannon still had a restlessness in her heart. She knew they were not right for each other. One day, Shannon received a job opportunity in another state. As she pondered her future, she realized it was the most difficult decision she ever had to make. She would have to leave the comfort of her home, her job, and her longtime boyfriend. For the first time in many years, she prayed. Ultimately, she decided to make the bold move and step decisively into the unknown. As hard as it was, she left everything that was familiar to her.

Shortly after her move, as she was making dinner in her new apartment, an overwhelming sense of loneliness and fear engulfed her. She began second-guessing her decision. As she sat there with tears in her eyes, God dropped the phrase "trust and obey" into her heart. She realized that it was time to rise up, let go of the hurt and pain from the past, and move forward into the future. As she made room for God in her life again and began attending church again, He began to heal and restore her. She experienced a great peace and comfort and was able to embrace the changes in her life, knowing that God was right there by her side. Before long, God opened doors for her to meet wonderful, new friends, and eventually she met and married her real "prince charming"—a man who truly surpassed her every expectation.

Shannon's restlessness was a result of God's trying to move her out of something that was not good for her into something new, positive, and healthy. It was her ability to recognize that something was wrong in her life, along with her willingness to trust God that gave her the courage to move forward.

Today, if you are in a relationship that is not right for you, don't wrestle with your feelings or make excuses for what's going on. I am not talking about a relationship already committed in marriage; I am talking about any relationship outside of marriage that you know is dragging you down and causing you to fall short of what you are intended to be. God has such a great desire for you to reach your full potential. Be willing to recognize if there is something wrong in your life, and have the courage to move forward with a new perspective. Today, be open for something bigger and better. Trust Him, because He wants you to have the right relationships and a strong, healthy future!

Scripture Reading: 2 Corinthians 6:14–18

 PRAYER FOR TODAY

Heavenly Father, I humbly come to You, trusting You with my relationships. I trust that You are connecting me with the right people to launch me forward into my destiny. Give me wisdom and discernment to let go of relationships that are not of You. I choose to keep my heart open so that I can move forward into the blessings that You have prepared for me. In Jesus' Name. Amen.

The Great Exchange

*He said to them, "Assuredly, I say to you, there is
no one who has left house or parents or brothers
or wife or children, for the sake of the kingdom of
God, who shall not receive many times more in this
present time, and in the age to come eternal life."*
Luke 18:29–30 (NKJV)

Everything we have in life happens by means of exchange. You exchange your time and talents for a paycheck. You exchange your paycheck for the things you need. Even a gift you might receive went through a process of exchange by someone at some point before it got to you. But by far, the greatest exchange of all time was over two thousand years ago when God exchanged our sin and brokenness for His righteousness. I love that old saying "I had a debt I could not pay; He paid a debt He did not owe."

Philippians 2 talks about working out our salvation. Salvation isn't a one-time event; it's a process. When you receive Jesus as your Lord and Savior, you begin that process. All throughout our walk of faith, we continually exchange ourselves, our attitudes, our ways, and our ideas for more of Him in our lives. We must never think we have "arrived," and we must always be willing to exchange what we have in our hands for what He has for us.

I heard a story about a little girl who was carefully saving her allowance money so she could buy something from the toy store. She didn't have much—only a few dollars—but one day she asked her daddy to take her to the store so she could buy something special. She was overwhelmed by endless aisles of shelves filled with games, dolls, and trinkets. Finally a particular item caught her eye, and she knew it was exactly what she wanted—a lovely strand of white, plastic pearls. She made her purchase and immediately went home to show off her treasure. She was so proud of that necklace; after all, she had saved up for it and picked it out all by herself. She wore it every day for several weeks. Her father saw this as an opportunity to teach his daughter about trust, so one day he asked her, "Honey, will you give me your pearls?"

"No, Daddy. I love my pearls!" she replied. "I can't give you my pearls!"

Her father didn't mention the pearl necklace for several days, and then he asked again, "Sweetie, do you trust me?"

"Yes, Daddy."

"Will you give me your pearls?"

And again she answered, "No, Daddy, I can't give you my pearls!"

Several more days passed, when the father went a third time to his daughter. "Do you trust me? Will you give me your pearls?"

Finally, with tears welling in her eyes, she reluctantly took off her beloved plastic pearls and handed them to her father. "Here, Daddy. You can have my pearls."

At that moment, the father pulled a small blue box from his pocket and handed it to his daughter. Her eyes grew wide with excitement as she opened the box to find the most gorgeous strand of genuine pearls. As the father fastened the pearls around her neck, he said, "I have had these special pearls for you all along; all you had to do was trust me."

Is there something you are holding on to today that is keeping you from God's best? If you'll let go of what's in your hand, an exchange will take place. God will let go of what's in His hand for you—peace, strength, wisdom, favor, and more! He'll give you exactly what you need. Don't settle for "plastic" when all you have to do is trust Him. Remember, He's taking you on a journey of faith, so open your hand and receive the beautiful strand of pearls God has for you today!

Scripture Reading: Luke 18:18–30

 PRAYER FOR TODAY

God in heaven, thank You for Your goodness and faithfulness to me. I choose to release everything I have in my hands to You. I trust that Your ways are better and Your thoughts are higher. I know that You are working behind the scenes on my behalf. Give me Your peace as I patiently wait on You. In Jesus' Name. Amen.

Chapter Four

Keeping the Right Perspective

New Attitude

Be constantly renewed in the spirit of your mind
[having a fresh mental and spiritual attitude].
Ephesians 4:23 (AMP)

Here in the South, it stays pretty warm almost year-round. I can't think of one indoor place in Houston that doesn't have air conditioning. I know up in the North it's a different story, but around here we are thankful for modern conveniences to help keep us cool! The thing about running the air conditioner so much is that you have to remember to change the air filter regularly; otherwise, it won't be long before the air flow is restricted, the unit is overworked, and it eventually burns out. There are lots of air conditioning repair companies who stay awfully busy in the summer months!

I find that our attitude is a lot like that air filter. When you have a new attitude, it filters out the "dust" of the world and protects your inner workings. In the same way that you regularly check your air filter, you have to constantly check your attitude and make sure it's not getting clogged up with negativity or restricting the flow of God's blessing. During those seasons of life when it feels like a heat wave of difficulty is coming against you, you have to be especially careful to keep your attitude fresh and change it as often as you need to. Many people go through life allowing their circumstances to dictate their attitudes; they don't realize that attitude is a choice. If you allow negative thinking into your life, it weighs you down and causes you to lose your joy and enthusiasm. Before long, you stop appreciating your friends and family; you start believing your boss has something against you. Negative thinking makes the small stuff seem so much bigger until you are living in constant worry and frustration. If that's how you feel today, take heart—your life can be different! Today, you can have a different outlook on life by making a simple choice.

One evening several years ago, I was sitting in my living room watching television when an advertisement came on showing a lovely young woman strolling down a sunny street. She was wearing a flowing dress, swinging her purse by her side, and all the while singing, "I've got a new attitude!" She was clearly enjoying her life and appeared as if she didn't have a care in the world. You could tell this woman wasn't naive. She wasn't on cloud nine because she was newly in love. She presented herself with a confidence that only comes by making it through some things. Yes, she looked as though she had fought some battles in her day and was enjoying the satisfaction of a recent victory. She was consciously making the most out of every moment.

I know it was just a commercial, but this woman looked as if she had the key to happiness in life! She looked as if she had that "new attitude" simply because she *chose* it. She wasn't going to allow her circumstances to dictate her joy and confidence. She was going to embrace each day and look for the best in life. It's funny that the commercial struck me so deeply, and I don't even remember what the product was, but one thing's for sure: I'll never forget the attitude of that woman!

What's your outlook on life today? Do you wake up every morning ready to embrace the day, or is it time to "change your filter"? Every day, life brings new opportunities and thousands of new choices. The first choice you get to make is about your attitude. When you choose to be grateful and approach the day with enthusiasm, you are "putting on" the right attitude. You are setting up your day for success and opening the door for you to be used by God in a powerful way!

Just like that woman in the commercial, you can choose your attitude each and every day. Not only that, but you have the power to influence people without even saying a word. I never met this woman, I never talked to her, she didn't do anything for me. I just saw her walking down the street in that commercial, and she had a lasting impact on me. How much more does your attitude and the way you approach your day influence the people around you! Today, put on a fresh, new mental attitude and embrace the blessings God has in store for you!

Scripture Reading: Philippians 4:4-8

PRAYER FOR TODAY

Dear Father, today I choose to put on a fresh, new mental attitude. I choose to be grateful and approach today with enthusiasm. I know that You have good things in store for me, and I open myself up to receive Your blessings. Direct my steps today as I keep my mind stayed on You. In Jesus' Name. Amen.

What Are You Magnifying?

O magnify the Lord with me, and let
us exalt His name together.
Psalm 34:3 (AMP)

When I was young, my dad used to keep a huge magnifying glass on his desk. My brother and I would borrow it and pretend that we were detectives ready to solve a mystery. We had so much fun with it! Of course, magnifying glasses aren't as popular as they used to be, but before the invention of eyeglasses, people used them quite often to read or to get a closer look at something. When you magnify something, you of course don't actually change the size of it, you change your *perspective* on it so that it appears larger to you.

Interestingly, our minds work a lot like a magnifying glass. The more you think about something, the larger you *perceive* it to be. When you focus intently on your situation, it doesn't actually change because of it, it just becomes larger and larger in your mind. Our lives go in the direction of our most dominant thoughts, which is why magnifying the wrong things can set your life on the wrong course in a hurry. We have to keep things in the right perspective and know when to put our "magnifying glass" down and stop dwelling on things we can't change. If you continue to focus on your problems, they can become so large in your mind that you can literally be consumed by them. But when you focus on God and magnify Him in your life, all the things of this world—the challenges, obstacles, and disappointments—just seem to melt away.

Here's another way to look at it: If you hold up a quarter in front of you with your arm outstretched and one eye closed, the quarter seems small compared to everything else you see around you. But if you pull that quarter closer to your eye, it appears much larger. In fact, if you hold it close enough, you won't be able to see anything else. This is what happens so often in life: difficulties and challenges seem so much larger than they actually are, simply because we hold them closer than necessary.

That's what happened to Eve in the book of Genesis. Eve was a woman who truly had it all. She was living in the most gorgeous and lush garden ever and she enjoyed magnificent streams, rivers, and waterfalls, all surrounded by the most fragrant and flourishing flowers, and she ate the most succulent fruits and veggies imaginable. Just think: no weight problems, no dirty laundry, and living with the perfect man—literally! Eve truly was in paradise. Until the day she began focusing her attention on the one thing in her garden that she couldn't have—the single forbidden fruit tree. I believe the more she looked at the fruit, the larger it became in her mind. She allowed that one tree to consume her thoughts and distort her perception of the entire garden. She no longer valued the treasures within her paradise. Instead, she magnified that one forbidden thing until it was so large in her mind's eye that she could see nothing else.

The wrong perspective will lead you down the wrong path, but changing your perspective can happen in a split second by simply changing your focus. To keep the right perspective, choose to magnify the right things in your life. When I come up against challenges, I remind myself of all the great things God has done for me. I begin to thank Him for allowing me to know Him; I thank Him for my family, my children, and my husband. I recall how God brought me through past trials and difficult times. I am always amazed at how my perspective changes when I have a grateful heart and choose to count my blessings!

Today, I encourage you to take inventory of your thoughts. You might want to make a list of all the things that are magnified in your life right now. Hold that list out in front of you and think about how big your God is! Ask Him to reveal Himself to you in greater ways. Sing a simple song of praise to Him as you release that list of cares into His loving arms. Remember, His yoke is easy and His burden is light. Magnify Him and watch the weight of the world disappear!

Scripture Reading: Proverbs 4:20–27

 PRAYER FOR TODAY

Father in heaven, I magnify You today. I lift You up and exalt You above anything else in my life. You alone are faithful and worthy of all praise. I choose to keep my mind focused on You and look for Your goodness. I bless You today and every day. In Jesus' Name. Amen.

Your Bags Are Packed

*My God will meet all your needs according
to his glorious riches in Christ Jesus.*
Philippians 4:19 (NIV)

Over the last five or six years, Joel and I have done a lot of traveling for ministry events, and I've packed a lot of suitcases,
which isn't exactly my favorite thing to do. I went through a season
in my life where it seemed like every time I turned around, I was
packing again. When I would go to close my suitcase, I would start
thinking, *Did I forget anything? Am I missing something?* I'd pull
everything out and check it twice. When the kids were younger, I'd
pack for them, too, and the thought of forgetting something they
needed had me triple checking. It got to the point where I started
dreading traveling and wondered if I should even go so much! I
thought, *Does Joel really need me to go? Will the people really notice
if I'm not there?*

So many people get anxious before they travel. They want to be
prepared, they don't want to miss their flights, and they want to
make sure they have everything they need when they reach their
destinations. In our spiritual journey, we want to be prepared, too.
We want to make sure we have everything we need to fulfill our

destiny. We want to be at the right place at the right time and connected with the right people.

It's good to have the drive and desire to fulfill your destiny, but you shouldn't be so focused on trying to "pack your bags" that it overshadows the enjoyment of your journey. In other words, you can't be so engrossed in the details, trying to orchestrate things, trying to make sure everything is perfect, that it keeps you from resting and trusting God. The truth in my situation was that it really wasn't that big of a deal if I forgot something. It wasn't like we were going anywhere where we couldn't get toothpaste, socks, or hairspray. But I had allowed my perspective to get out of balance in this area, and of course when I realized how absurd and out of character my thinking had become, I quickly made a few adjustments to focus on the right things!

Today, I want to encourage you to relax and enjoy the journey of life, because your bags are already packed. God Himself is handling the details of your journey. He's thought of everything and He's left nothing out. You have what you need today, and anything you'll need when you reach your next destination, He will provide for you. Find rest in Him, knowing that He will supply all your needs according to His riches in glory.

Scripture Reading: Matthew 6:25–34

⌒◦﹏◦⌒ PRAYER FOR TODAY ⌒◦﹏◦⌒

Heavenly Father, thank You for providing everything I need for this journey of life. I trust that You are handling the details, arranging the right opportunities and the right connections, and ordering my steps. I choose to rest in You because You are faithful. I look forward with anticipation to what You have prepared for me. In Jesus' Name. Amen.

Big-Picture Thinking

*We fix our eyes not on what is seen,
but on what is unseen. For what is seen is
temporary, but what is unseen is eternal.*
2 *Corinthians 4:18 (NIV)*

There's a story I share in my book *Love Your Life* about a friend of mine who was showing me pictures from her recent vacation. She had just returned from a wonderful cruise that her entire family had been saving for and planning for months. This trip was especially meaningful because she was able to spend time with members of her extended family that she hadn't seen in over a year.

When she returned from her trip, we decided to meet for lunch with a group of friends to welcome her back home. She was the last to arrive at the restaurant and was all smiles as she walked over to the table with her new photos in hand. "Would you like to see the pictures I just picked up from my family vacation? I haven't even had a chance to look at them myself yet."

"Of course!" we all said. We were happy to share in her excitement and began passing around the photos. They were filled with images of the fabulous cruise ship, beautiful sandy beaches, charming island shops, and lots of happy faces. But before long, I noticed an uncomfortable expression on my friend's face; then she began to complain about her appearance in the pictures. "Oh, I didn't know I looked like that! This picture is awful!" She had something negative to say about herself in every print. Just a few moments earlier, she was so excited, but as soon as she changed her focus to what she saw as her flaws, she completely lost her joy and missed the beauty of reliving those wonderful moments with us. Instead of enjoying the memory of the marvelous trip with her family, she lost her enthusiasm as she focused on her imperfections—little things that only she could see.

We all have times when it's difficult to see the big picture of life because we single out what we consider to be wrong about our lives. Maybe you're in a job you don't like, or perhaps you're trying to sell your home. Maybe a relationship isn't working out the way you had hoped, or you've experienced a significant loss. These are challenging circumstances to face, but the truth is, in the big picture of eternity, these things are only temporary. We have the choice to either zero in on our difficulties, or take a step back and look at the big picture of life.

We have to remember that life isn't just about what we can see. There's another dimension to our existence—and that is eternity. Eternity is happening right now, and our earthly lives parallel it. I love what the psalmist said in Psalm 121: "I lift up my eyes . . ." He knew that if he stayed focused on his circumstances, his circumstances were going to drag him down. Instead, he looked up at the big picture of his life, knowing that God had more for him than what he could see in this natural realm. The same is true for us— when we lift up our eyes to the big picture, we can better appreciate what God is doing now and what He wants to do in the future.

Today, I encourage you to take a step back and look at the big picture of your life and all the wonderful blessings that surround you. Recall to mind all the good things God has done for you, and don't let the little imperfections of this temporary life steal your joy or rob you of His blessings.

Remember my friend with the vacation photos? You know, I'm sure she'll look back on those pictures thirty years from now and think, *Wow, I looked pretty good!* Don't wait thirty years to start appreciating what you have. Start looking at the goodness in your life today, because there's so much more to this existence when you look at the big picture of life!

Scripture Reading: Psalm 121:1–8

PRAYER FOR TODAY

Heavenly Father, today I lift up my eyes to You and choose to focus on the big picture of life. I know that You are working behind the scenes, orchestrating my every step. Help me, by Your Spirit, to keep the right perspective. In Jesus' Name. Amen.

Finding Contentment

I know what it is to be in need, and I know what
it is to have plenty. I have learned the secret of
being content in any and every situation.
Philippians 4:12 (NIV)

Finding contentment is a goal we should strive for each and every day. Some people get confused about the concept of contentment because they think it means they have to settle where they are, or just sit back and go with the flow. However, there's a huge difference between being content and being complacent. When you are content, you are satisfied; you're full. It's not that you aren't pursuing your goals or striving to reach new levels; you are just able to enjoy where you are on the way to where you are going.

For example, everyone knows that if you send a woman to the mall to buy a new sweater, she might stroll through fourteen different stores while she's there. She keeps her "mission" on the backburner of her mind, content to browse the stores and enjoy her journey. Most men, on the other hand, can't understand at all why a woman would spend all that time wandering around! A man's approach would be to get in and out of the mall in ten minutes— eight if he's been to that store before and knows his way around. That's because most men are more mission-minded. They focus on the goal, whereas most women focus on the experience. The truth is, we have to have both. We have to be mission-minded *and* enjoy ourselves on the way to reaching our goals.

One of the best ways I know to find contentment in your circumstances is to reach out and help someone in need. There's always someone in your life who needs what you have to give. When you turn your focus toward helping others, your own challenges seem more manageable, and sometimes they simply disappear.

Linda was a young woman who seemed to have a great life, a thriving career, and a devoted circle of friends; but Linda wanted to lose twenty-five pounds that she gained after her divorce two years earlier. She tried just about everything and was overwhelmed by this mountain in front of her. She stopped going out so much and wasn't able to enjoy her friends. She felt defeated and intimidated every time she would try to go to the gym. On the weekends, she would usually wind up on the sofa, watching television with her two best friends, Ben and Jerry—chocolate fudge brownie, of course! She finally decided to join a structured weight-loss program as a last-ditch effort to regain control of her life.

The night she arrived at her first meeting, she was both nervous and excited about finding a solution to her all-consuming weight issue. *Finally! I can get rid of this weight and be happy*, she thought. As she walked in, she saw an empty seat next to a woman wearing a long, casual dress. She introduced herself and immediately began telling the woman about how she couldn't wait to lose her weight so she could feel comfortable at the gym again or wear a bathing suit and enjoy waterskiing. Realizing that she was dominating the conversation, Linda stopped and asked the woman, "What made you decide to join the program?" The woman replied, "Several years ago, I was in a terrible car accident and almost lost my life. I was so depressed after spending weeks in the hospital, all I could do was find comfort in food. Now, I've gained so much weight that I can't wear the prosthetic leg I received after I lost my own leg in the accident. As soon as I get this weight off, I'm going to be able to fit into my prosthetic leg so I can walk again."

As Linda listened to the woman's story, her eyes welled up with tears. At that moment, Linda realized that her "problem" was hardly a problem at all compared to what this woman was facing. Linda was determined to help her newfound friend in any way she could. She agreed to call her several times throughout the week and encourage her to stay on track. She went over to her house and took her out for walks in the sunshine. Over time, Linda was able to see the women reach her goal and finally wear her prosthetic leg. But something else happened along the way. Linda became totally content with where she was in life. As she encouraged the woman, she found encouragement for herself! It wasn't long before Linda reached her goal—and it seemed almost effortless.

Today, I encourage you to find contentment in your journey by reaching out to others. What you make happen for other people, God will make happen for you. There's always someone who can draw from the strength that you have when you take your eyes off your own problems and help someone else through theirs.

Scripture Reading: Psalm 119:57–64

 PRAYER FOR TODAY

Dear God, thank You for another day to worship You. Today, I take my eyes off my own circumstances and choose to reach out to help others. I invite You to bring people into my life whom I can bless and encourage. As I obey Your Word, I know that I will find contentment and satisfaction all the days of my life. In Jesus' Name. Amen.

Avoid Exaggerated Thinking

*Dear friend, guard Clear Thinking and Common Sense
with your life; don't for a minute lose sight of them.*
Proverbs 3:21 (MSG)

We all go through seasons when we feel overwhelmed by circumstances in life. When this happens, it's easy for your thinking to get off track and out of balance. Your thoughts can start to become more exaggerated, which stifles your ability to find solutions. In order to keep a balanced perspective and move forward in your life, you have to learn to recognize and avoid exaggerated thinking.

Exaggerated thinking makes a bigger deal out of things than the reality calls for. It's demonstrated when we talk ourselves out of doing something simple because we've convinced ourselves that it's going to take so much more effort than it actually will. Exaggerated thinking says, *I'm never going to get a better job. I'm never going to get married. I'll never lose this weight. I'll never get out of debt.* Sound familiar? Thinking in extremes like this narrows your focus and actually limits God and blocks the flow of His blessings. On top of that, when exaggerated thinking creeps in, it can cause us to miss opportunities and important moments with family and loved ones.

One afternoon, years ago, Alexandra asked me if I could take her to the mall. I had some things to do around the house that day and thought there was no way I could fit a trip to the mall into my schedule. Well, it happened to be Joel's day off, so he decided to take Alexandra on a father-daughter outing. They made plans to go to Build-A-Bear Workshop and then have lunch. I kissed them good-bye, and as they drove off, I started on my projects, thinking that I would have all afternoon to myself. About an hour and forty-five minutes later, Joel and Alexandra were pulling back into the driveway. I thought for sure that something was wrong. But then I saw the bear in Alexandra's arms, so I knew they had at least made it to the mall. When Alexandra came into the house, I asked, "Did you and Daddy have a good time?"

"Yes," she gushed excitedly.

"Did you eat lunch?" I asked, thinking she'd be hungry.

"Oh, yes," Alexandra replied. "And Daddy took me to the candy store for my dessert."

I couldn't believe it! In my mind, that trip should have taken four hours or more. I would have had to clear my calendar for the whole afternoon, but Alexandra was just happy that she was able to spend some quality time with her daddy. She didn't care about making a big "to-do" out of everything. After a short time, she was ready to come home anyway.

How often do we put off important things because we make them bigger in our minds than they really are? You think you can't do "this" or "that" because you think you need to schedule it far in advance, or you can't go somewhere because you don't have the right clothes. Maybe you feel like you can't invite your friends and family over because the dining room needs painting, the gutters need fixing, or your silverware doesn't match. The truth is, no one is ever going to remember your forks or the gutters! What they will remember is the quality time spent with those who care about them. Don't exaggerate the importance of the little things so much that you miss out on the joy of what really matters! We've all seen the mother who obsesses so much over her child's birthday party that she forgets to stop and enjoy her own child!

How many moments have you missed because you were so wrapped up in making everything perfect? We've all been there, and most of the time our frustration stems from our sincere desire to bless the people we love, but we have to remember to keep a balanced perspective. Everything doesn't have to be perfect before you can enjoy life. Maybe all that your child or loved one wants is for you to throw a blanket in the backyard and have a simple picnic. Sure, something will always come up, but most things can wait. The laundry can wait, the phone can wait, and the dishes can wait, but your loved ones need your investment of time and attention. Don't let exaggerated thinking keep you from enjoying the people in your life. Remember, no one gets to the end of life and says, "Boy, I sure do wish I had worked more hours in the office," or, "I wish I would have had a cleaner house." No, at the end of their lives, most people say, "I wish I would have spent more time with my family and loved ones." Choose to avoid exaggerated thinking so you can embrace all the wonderful experiences life affords you today.

Scripture Reading: Proverbs 3:21–26

 PRAYER FOR TODAY

Heavenly Father, thank You for the gift of today. I don't want to miss a single moment of blessing. Help me to recognize exaggerated thinking so I can keep the proper perspective. Give me creative ways to bless the people I love today so I can enjoy all the wonderful blessings You have for me. In Jesus' Name. Amen.

Find Joy in Difficult Times

Count it all joy when you fall into various trials,
knowing that the testing of your faith produces patience.
But let patience have its perfect work,
that you may be perfect and complete,
lacking nothing.

James 1:2–4 (NKJV)

The most rewarding relationships are built and proven over time. They take effort, investment, and self-sacrifice. But sadly, when it comes to facing challenges in relationships, our culture today makes it easy to focus on the short term, seeking self-gratification rather than considering the long-term value of the investment made in that relationship.

It's sort of like buying a house; over time you build equity. Sometimes, it takes longer than you anticipated. Sometimes the market is down, sometimes it's up. Sometimes you see houses that you think you'd like better. But if you'll keep being faithful, if you'll keep making those payments and taking care of your investment, it will pay off in a big way down the road.

The same is true in relationships. We have to keep the right perspective and keep investing in what we have. Think about this: If you had a beautiful house with $50,000 in equity and then discovered a $1,500 plumbing problem, it may seem like a big deal, but compared to what you have invested, it's really a rather small problem. You wouldn't just turn your house keys over to the bank and walk away from it over a $1,500 issue. No, you'd figure out some way to get that repair done. You might get a second job or work out a payment arrangement. Either way, you would make the effort to get that problem fixed so you could live comfortably in your house and protect your investment. In homeownership, it's easy to get bent out of shape over a problem like a roof leak, but that can be repaired. Instead, why not focus your energy on being thankful that you have a roof over your head! The same principle is true in relationships. Many of the day-to-day annoyances may get us bent out of shape. It may cost us something to repair a relationship—it may cost our pride, it may cost some time and effort, it may even cost going to get some professional help, but it won't cost nearly as much as what you would lose if you walked away. In the Bible, James says that we should count it all joy when we encounter trials. Notice he didn't say "if" we encounter trials or difficulty. No, every person on this planet is guaranteed to face some challenges, obstacles, and adversity—especially in relationships. We all have times when our expectations aren't met or a friend lets us down or things just don't turn out the way we planned. But we can't let those challenges become stumbling blocks that destroy our relationships and affect our faith. Instead, we have to turn them into stepping stones that draw us closer to God and strengthen our relationships.

Every trial, every adversity, is a defining moment in our lives. Those difficulties can either hold us back, or they can propel us forward into the good things God has for us. We decide how those things will affect our lives. If we choose to be bitter and upset, constantly complaining about what's happening, then we aren't going to get very far. But if we choose to have a positive attitude of faith, if we choose to find joy even in the midst of our trials, we can move forward in His peace and joy. I love what James says will happen next: when we allow patience to work in our lives, we become complete, lacking nothing! That's why we can "count it all joy"—

because on the other side of that difficulty is a place of wholeness, abundance, and victory!

I encourage you to take a step back and look at what you have invested in your relationships. Maybe you're facing some difficult times, but consider all you've come through so far. What's the value of the time, energy, heart, and commitment you've invested? Instead of focusing on the problems, choose to focus on the treasure of the relationship. Focus on the future. Focus on allowing patience to have its perfect work. When you get the right perspective regarding relationships, those frustrations and challenges seem much more manageable.

Today, no matter what you may be going through, make sure you keep the right attitude. Find joy in the midst of your difficulty, knowing that it's only temporary. Keep your eyes focused straight ahead and keep moving forward, because there is a place of victory and abundance waiting for you.

Scripture Reading: James 1:2–12

 PRAYER FOR TODAY

Heavenly Father, today I choose joy. I choose peace. I choose to stand strong even in the difficult times. Help me to keep my eyes on the investments I have in my relationships. Teach me to love the way You love and to overlook offenses. In Jesus' Name. Amen.

Push Your Thoughts Around

We take captive every thought to make it obedient to Christ.
2 Corinthians 10:5 (NIV)

One afternoon I was having a late lunch with a friend at a nice restaurant. Throughout the lunch I noticed my friend was becoming increasingly irritated with our waiter who was somewhat forgetful, inattentive, and slow. I really couldn't believe the way my friend was acting. It was pretty out of character. I just chuckled as I asked her why she was allowing the waiter to get her so worked up. She told me, "I have a hard time dealing with people who are just plain slow. I get frustrated when people are lollygagging and only doing their job halfheartedly. Sometimes, I get so irritated that I blurt out something that I know I shouldn't say. Then I get mad at myself for doing it!"

I could tell immediately that she needed to change her perspective, so I asked her, "What are you thinking about right now? Are you keeping score of all his mistakes?"

She began to laugh and said, "Yes, that's exactly what I am doing."

I said, "Are his mistakes really worth this whole lunch? Are they so important that those mistakes deserve more of your attention than I do?"

She quickly got the message and decided that instead of allowing her circumstances to dictate her thoughts, she was going to choose her thoughts more carefully.

Do you ever find yourself getting frustrated at people like my friend did? Are you keeping score at the grocery-store checkout? What's going through your mind when that coworker who always seems to annoy you approaches you during lunch? Are you thinking, *Here we go again*? When you go back into your memory and retrieve past frustrations, you are setting yourself up to relive them. We have to be conscious of every thought and be careful of what we choose to dwell on.

I heard a story about a little girl who whined and complained about everything one day. The next day, she was cheerful and sweet to everyone. Her mother said, "Yesterday, you had such a bad attitude. Today, you're so happy about everything. What happened?"

The little girl replied, "Yesterday my thoughts were pushing me around. Today I'm pushing my thoughts around."

Just like this little girl, we have to take control of every thought. Don't let negative thoughts play over in your head and cause you to say and do things you will regret later. Instead of keeping score, keep a positive attitude. When it comes to those little irritations, let people off the hook by looking for the best in them. When you do, you influence others to do the same. Do you ever notice that when you have a negative perspective about someone, it doesn't take long before the people around you do too?

There was a husband and wife who were always talking negatively about his mother, not thinking about the fact that their four-year-old daughter was hearing everything they were saying. They assumed that because she was so young, it didn't matter, but whenever Grandma would come over, the little girl would pull back and try to hide. The couple had to urge their daughter to "Go hug Grandma." Overhearing her parents' negative conversations affected the way she felt about her grandma.

Remember, your words have power to influence people. Don't sow discord; sow peace. Don't let your thoughts push you around;

instead push your thoughts around! Choose to see the best in others, because when you magnify the good, the good will increase and bring a harvest of blessing in return.

Scripture Reading: Philippians 2:12–18

⟬⟭ PRAYER FOR TODAY ⟬⟭

Heavenly Father, today I choose to glorify You with my thoughts, attitudes, and actions. I take captive every thought and make it obedient to Your Word. I choose to bless others and extend grace to the people around me, knowing that You will extend Your grace to me in return. In Jesus' Name. Amen.

How Do You See the Glass?

*Give thanks in all circumstances, for this
is God's will for you in Christ Jesus.*
1 Thessalonians 5:18 (NIV)

One day a few years back, I was working in the living room while Alexandra was playing nearby. I was starting to get thirsty and didn't want to lose my place in what I was doing, so I asked Alexandra if she would get me a glass of water. She jumped up, ran into the kitchen, and came back and handed me a glass *half* filled with water and quickly went straight back to playing.

I sat there for a moment looking at the glass in my hand and chuckled as I thought about a simple life lesson. At that moment, I was expecting Alexandra to bring me a full glass of water. I thought about that glass of water, I envisioned it, I certainly wanted it, and in my mind, I clearly communicated my wish to Alexandra. But sometimes, no matter how hard we try, no matter what we do, no matter what we think should happen, *life doesn't always give us what we are expecting.* In fact, many times in life we get served "half a glass of water," or less than what we were expecting. When this happens, we have a choice to make. Now, for me it was just a glass of water, but what happens when you don't get that promotion you hoped for? What happens when a loved one leaves your life?

What happens when you work so hard for something and it falls through?

So often, people allow those unmet expectations to become their focus, which can quickly turn into a black hole of negative, self-defeated thinking. Once you allow your thoughts to follow that path, it becomes very difficult to turn your thinking, and your life, around. The good news is that we don't have to let our thoughts take that route. When things don't go our way, we have the power to choose how we will respond. You choose your perspective. You can either focus on what you didn't get, or you can focus on what you have in your hand. It may not be what you expected, but God can use it in your life if you'll allow Him to.

Instead of getting upset about what I didn't have that day, I chose to be thankful for what I did have. After all, it was certainly more water than I had a few minutes earlier! The glass was half empty, but it was also half full.

Today, let me encourage you to get up every day and focus on what you do have in life. Be thankful for the blessing of the little things, even when you don't get what you expect. Keep seeking God, because He is faithful and He is a rewarder of those who diligently seek Him. His delay is not His denial. We have to trust that He knows what's best for us and that His timing is perfect. Even when things don't make sense in the natural, remember that He is working behind the scenes for your good. Your part is to keep your mind and heart focused in the right direction and approach each day with faith and gratitude. A positive person sees the best in every situation and uses her energy to bring solutions to life's challenges. Today, see the glass as half full and let your positive attitude empower you to live life to the fullest and enjoy the abundant life He has promised you!

Scripture Reading: Philippians 4:4–9

PRAYER FOR TODAY

Father in heaven, thank You for blessing my life in so many wonderful ways. Today, I release my unmet expectations and trust that You are ordering my steps. Even when things don't go my way, I choose to believe that You are at work in my life. Help me to always see Your hand moving on my behalf. In Jesus' Name. Amen.

Chapter Five

Making the Most of
What You Have

Put Action Behind Your Faith

*As the body without the spirit is dead,
so faith without works is dead also.*

James 2:26 (NKJV)

So many people today are living far below their God-given potential. They've put their dreams on hold because of past disappointments or setbacks. They've settled where they are, still hoping
that one day something will happen. They let the days slip by, all
the while harboring their dreams silently in their hearts.

But God did not create us to live this way. We were never meant
to just go through the motions of life. We aren't meant to just sur-
vive; we are meant to thrive. We were born to pursue our dreams
and see those dreams fulfilled! However, it's not going to just automatically happen; we have to do our part. The Bible says that faith
without works is dead. In other words, we have to step out and do
something if we're going to see our dreams fulfilled. We have to
prepare ourselves and be ready for the open doors God sets before
us. We have to take action if we truly want to see those dreams and
desires come to pass.

When I was a young girl in elementary school, I had a shy personality, yet I always felt like there was something big on the inside
of me. I was a dreamer with a vivid imagination. When it came

time for the fifth-grade school play, I really wanted the lead role; however, I didn't step up to make my teacher aware of it. The day came for the teacher to announce who would play the lead, and, of course, she didn't pick me, *the shy girl*; instead, she picked one of my classmates. Naturally, I was disappointed, but even back then I was filled with hope and imagined that somehow that little girl wouldn't be able to play the role after all. Perhaps she would have to go out of town with her family, and there I would be, standing in the wings when my "big moment" came! The teacher would *have to* pick me after all. Yes, in my mind I dreamed of getting the big part, and although it never happened, I rehearsed that scenario over and over in my mind, wishing that I could play the lead.

Years later I realized that although I had been dreaming about playing the lead, I didn't take action. I didn't rehearse the lines or memorize the scenes. I didn't stay after school for the voluntary practices. Sure, I *desired* to play the role, but I certainly wasn't *preparing* for it. Had the teacher called on me, I wouldn't have been ready to walk through that door of opportunity. Being filled with hope and expectation is a great place to start, but it's also a poor place to stop.

How often do we "sit in the wings" of life, wishing we were doing more, believing that we have more in us, waiting for our big moment? Yet, if opportunity were to knock on our door, we might not even be ready. If you are really believing and expecting for big things to happen, you have to put action behind your faith and live your life ready to make the most of every opportunity. I've heard it said that *success happens when preparation meets opportunity.* That's why it is important to use and develop your gifts and talents so when opportunity presents itself, you will have the confidence to walk through that open door.

Today, think about some of the things you can do to prepare yourself to take hold of a dream. Do you desire to change careers? Maybe you need to take some classes or find a mentor in that field. Do you desire to be married or improve your marriage relationship? Be the best "you" that you can be. Take care of yourself physically and emotionally so you can offer strength to your relationships. Be faithful with what's in your hand and God will bless it. Put action behind your faith and get ready, because He is going to open up doors of opportunity before you!

Scripture Reading: James 2:14-24

 PRAYER FOR TODAY

Heavenly Father, thank You for the privilege of being Your child. Thank You for the gifts, talents, and abilities that You've placed inside of me. Show me how to put actions behind my faith and prepare myself for the open doors You have in store for my future. In Jesus' Name. Amen.

Look for Success in Every Day

*Keep on asking, and you will receive what you ask
for. Keep on seeking, and you will find. Keep on
knocking, and the door will be opened to you.*
Matthew 7:7 (NLT)

Your thoughts, attitudes, and words operate like magnets. Whatever you are looking for, whatever you are dwelling on, is what you will draw into your life. Scripture tells us that when you operate out of an attitude of fear, you will draw negative things into your life. However, when you operate with an attitude of faith and expectancy, you'll draw in the good that God desires for you. That's why it's so important to look for success in every day. Not every day is going to be perfect, but whatever you focus on sets you up to take a step toward victory and blessing, or frustration and defeat. For example, maybe today you cheated on your diet or said something you wish you hadn't. You can either focus on those setbacks, or you can thank God that you recognized them and are now taking steps in the right direction. You can either focus on your mistakes or focus on your milestones. The question is, do you want to set yourself up for more mistakes, or do you want to set yourself up for more milestones!

Think about where you set your focus when you are driving

a car. You wouldn't get into your car first thing in the morning, buckle your seat belt, adjust your mirrors, put the car in reverse, and step on the gas while you are still facing forward, looking out your windshield at your garage. That would be crazy! Nor would you enter the freeway going sixty-five while you are turned around in your seat, watching the traffic come up behind you. In either scenario, you'd be headed for trouble in a jiffy. The same is true in life. You have to look in the direction you want to go. If you want to move forward, you have to look forward. If you want to see success in your future, look for success in each and every day—no matter how big or small it may seem.

Not only can you look for success in your own life, but you can look for it in the lives of other people. When you look for the good in others and applaud them for their accomplishments, you are sowing seed. You know that old saying "What goes around comes around"? That's actually a biblical principle dating all the way back to the book of Genesis. God set up a system of sowing and reaping, and our future is set by the seeds we sow today! Finding success in others will set you up for success down the road too.

Remember, even though you've made some wrong decisions in your life, you've made a whole lot of right decisions too. Maybe you didn't get everything done that you wanted to yesterday, but at least you're making progress! You're better off than you were in your past, and your future is getting brighter and brighter. The fact that you are holding this devotional in your hand right now shows that you have a desire to start your day off in the direction of success. Acknowledge it and applaud yourself for it. Look in the direction you want your life to go. See yourself blessed and successful in your mind's eye, and watch the blessing of God unfold in every area of your life.

Scripture Reading: Luke 11:9–13

PRAYER FOR TODAY

Father God, today I choose to set my focus in the direction of success. You said in Your Word that what I seek, I will find, and so I choose to look for the good in today both in myself and in the people around me. Strengthen me, by Your Spirit, as I keep my heart and mind focused on You. In Jesus' Name. Amen.

Making the Most of What You Have

Please don't squander one bit of this
marvelous life God has given us.
2 *Corinthians 6:1 (MSG)*

God has given you a marvelous life here on earth! Sometimes you may not see it, but He's equipped you with everything you need to accomplish your dreams and fulfill your purpose. Scripture says, "To those who have, more will be given." That means when you use what you've been given, when you make the most of what you have in your hand, you will tap into more gifts, talents, and opportunities.

Jesus told a story about a wealthy man who entrusted some of his money, called *talents* in Bible days, to three of his employees. He instructed them to invest the talents and make the most of what he had given them, and then he went away on a business trip. Upon his return, he found that two of the men used their talents wisely and doubled the return on their investments. However, one man said, "I buried my talent because I was afraid." This man was full of excuses, trying to explain why he didn't do anything constructive with what he was given. Perhaps the man thought he didn't have any good contacts, or maybe he was busy taking care of other issues. Regardless, the wealthy man asked, "Couldn't you have at least put my money into a savings account so it could draw interest?" The employer was so frustrated that he took back what he had given to that man and gave it to the first man who had been so faithful. It's interesting that *all* the men had the same opportunity, but the third man, who was full of excuses, didn't take advantage of it.

In the same way that the wealthy man in the parable entrusted talents to the three men, God has also entrusted every person with a measure of gifts, talents, and abilities. He's watching to see what we will do with them. If you are faithful with what He has given you, He will multiply you and increase you in ways you never dreamed. It's not about how much you have; it's about *using* what you have. God is a faithful God, and He is looking for people to be faithful with what He has entrusted to them. We can't allow excuses to cause us to bury what we have been given. The wealthy man in the parable wasn't moved by excuses, and neither is God. God is moved by our faith in Him. When we trust in His goodness and act upon His Word, we are opening the door for Him to pour out His supernatural blessing upon us.

Today, look for ways to use what God has placed in your hands. Don't bury your talents. Believe in yourself, and believe that God is working on your behalf. Use what He has given You, and trust that He will bring increase. It may not happen right away, but if you will stay in faith and make the most of what you have, it won't be long until you see His hand of blessing upon every area of your life.

Scripture Reading: Ephesians 5:15–20

 PRAYER FOR TODAY

Heavenly Father, thank You for entrusting me with Your talents, abilities, and resources. I choose to be a faithful steward and make the most of what You have given me. Direct my steps and show me where to invest what you have placed in my hand. In Jesus' Name. Amen.

Look for a Sign

I do believe; help me overcome my unbelief!
Mark 9:24 (NIV)

Sometimes when opportunities come our way, we think, *I can't do that*, or, *That's impossible.* We talk ourselves out of it before we have a chance to even try it. We make so many excuses that we eventually start living those excuses as if they were the truth and we never even explore other possibilities.

One day I was having a conversation with a friend who was encouraging me to step out and do a particular thing. Before I even thought twice about it, I blurted out, "Oh, I can't do that!" It wasn't because I didn't *want* to do it; I had just made excuses about doing it for so long that I convinced myself that I couldn't. Later on, I thought to myself, *Why can't I do that? Maybe I really can do that.* I realized that up until that point I had a DO NOT ENTER sign hanging at the door of my mind regarding that area. I didn't even stop to consider how I could do it; all I saw was DO NOT ENTER. In my mind, we were just not going there!

Have you ever heard yourself say, "I can't do that; I am not that talented; I don't have the finances," or "I haven't done that in so long, I am too old; I am too out of shape." If you have, you might need to remove a DO NOT ENTER sign from your own thinking! It's easy to think, *I'm never going to get married. I've been divorced for too long.* Or, *I'm never going to get out of debt. I owe too much money.* Don't allow yourself to make excuses, because if you make them long enough, you may start to believe them. Instead, keep God's promises in the forefront of your thinking. Invite Him into every area of your life. Have the attitude, *I may not have met the right person yet, but I will. I'm going to focus my efforts on being the right kind of person so when God opens that door, I will be ready.* Or say, "I may not see how I could ever get out of debt, but I know God says I am blessed, and as I do my part, God will help me." Maybe you are saying, "I have been overweight for so long, I could never look like I did when I got married." Take down that DO NOT ENTER sign, because God wants to show Himself strong in every area of your life.

Jesus said in Revelation 3, "I stand at the door of your heart and knock." Did you know this scripture was written to people who already knew the Lord? Jesus is saying in this verse, "Please let me into every area of your life. Please trust that I can do more than you could ever think or imagine. Will you take down the DO NOT ENTER sign?"

Today, if you're recognizing some areas of your life in which you need to be more open, just choose to make the change. Don't let condemnation or guilt creep in, because everyone faces areas where they need to make more room for God in their thinking. Remember Moses? Yes, the great man of God also started out with a DO NOT ENTER sign in his mind. When God called him to lead the Hebrew people out of captivity, the first statement out of his mouth was, "I can't, God; I stutter." Moses sincerely wanted to help the Israelites, but he'd made so many excuses that he didn't believe in himself. But God wanted to help Moses. He wanted to empower him, so He told Moses, "I will send your brother, Aaron, to help you."

Just as God helped Moses, He wants to help you accomplish great things in your life. If you will take down the DO NOT ENTER signs and try again, He will be right there, ready, willing, and able to empower you and equip you. He will bring the right people across your path and open new doors in front of you. Trust Him with every area of your life because He is faithful. Open up your thinking, take down the DO NOT ENTER signs, and get ready for the amazing things He will do in your life!

Scripture Reading: Mark 9:20–24

 PRAYER FOR TODAY

Father in heaven, today I come humbly to Your throne of grace. Search my heart and mind, and reveal to me any areas where I may have a DO NOT ENTER sign in my thinking. Today, I choose to release old mind-sets so that I can receive everything You have in store for my future. In Jesus' Name. Amen.

Passing the Faithfulness Test

He who is faithful in what is least is faithful also in much.
Luke 16:10 (NKJV)

Sometimes God presents opportunities that look small or insignificant, maybe even ordinary. Perhaps you don't see how they fit into the big picture of your life at first. However, if God is presenting you with something, He has a purpose for it. He has a plan to use it in your life to increase you and promote you to larger responsibilities through it.

For many years, Joel's father had a hair stylist who would help him make sure he looked his best before he ministered. One day she wasn't able to do that job anymore, and I happened to be standing there when she announced her resignation. Joel's father immediately turned to me and asked if I would take her place. Now, I wasn't a hairdresser. I didn't go to cosmetology school. My first thought was, *If you're bold enough to trust me, I'm bold enough to do it. It's your hair!* Even though I didn't feel qualified, I remembered that I did have *some* experience. It's nothing I would ever list on a resume, but when I was a young girl, maybe thirteen or fourteen years old, my friends in the neighborhood would come over, and we would all go out to the garage where I would cut and style their hair. What started as simple haircuts turned into coloring and highlighting. I practically had my own neighborhood beauty shop right in our garage! As insignificant as it seemed, it was enough to give me the confidence to take the position as my father-in-law's stylist.

Joel's father used to tell us that he was going to preach into his nineties, and I had no reason to believe any differently. I remember one day I was calculating how old I would be, still doing Daddy's hair when he was ninety, and I can tell you it would have been a long time! Nevertheless, I was committed. I said to God, *If this is what You have for me to do, I am going to be the most faithful person You can find. I am going to stick with this even when there are other things I would like to be doing.*

And believe me, there were a lot of other things I could have been doing on the weekends, but I was committed, even though it was difficult to see how this fit into the big picture of my life. I had no idea where this could possibly take me. But when I didn't understand or when I would start to question in my mind, one scripture always came to my heart: *If you will be faithful in the little, God will trust you with much more.*

God needs us to pass the faithfulness test so He can pour greater things into us. If you want to grow and increase in any area of your life, you have to use what you have been given; then God will multiply it. If you want to grow in discipline, start being on time everywhere you go. If you want to get in better physical shape, take a walk for some exercise. If you want that promotion at work, do your best at your current job, and God will increase you. Don't wait around for the big moment; faithfulness starts where you are today. If you have the gift of singing, don't wait around for Sony Records to sign you; start singing in your church choir. You never know what door God will open for you as you begin to use what you have.

As I look back over my time with Daddy Osteen, or "The Big O" as I used to call him, I wouldn't trade it for the world. I loved him, and he loved me. We had a bond that I will always cherish. During that season, I learned so much about ministry. It was as if I was enrolled in a ministry mentorship program and didn't even realize it! I believe that if it were not for those years we spent together, I would not have the same opportunities I have today.

Remember, when you are faithful to God, He will be faithful to you. He always has your best interest at heart, and He is working all things together for your good. Be faithful with what you have in your hand, no matter how small, because God is using it to do something mighty in your life.

Scripture Reading: 2 Peter 1:3–8

 PRAYER FOR TODAY

Heavenly Father, I thank You for the blessing of today. Thank You for every good and perfect gift that You have placed in my hand. I choose to be faithful with what You have entrusted to me. I know that You are using what You have given me to grow me and equip me for the good things You have in store for my future. In Jesus' Name. Amen.

Pour In What You Have

He refused to drink it; instead,
he poured it out to the LORD.
1 *Chronicles 11:18 (NIV)*

Life is lived one day at a time, and the way to prepare for to-morrow is to live at your very best today. Whether you want to further your career or change some bad habits, if you'll do what you know to do today, God will help you get to where you need to be tomorrow. Don't fall into the trap of thinking, *When my boss recognizes my talent, then I will start doing my best work*, or, *As soon as I get another job, then I will be happy*, or perhaps, *When my children grow up, then I can pursue my dreams*. No, don't put your life on hold until the *big moment*; start living today, because every day lived well is one day closer to accomplishing your dreams. Start pouring in what you have and doing what you know to do, and God will use it for your good.

There's an old story about a traveler who hiked for many miles across the desert mountains. His water supply was gone, and he knew that if he didn't find water soon, he would surely die. In the distance, he noticed an abandoned cabin and hoped to find some water there. Once he made it to the cabin, he discovered an old well. There was a tin can tied to the pump with a note inside that read:

> Dear stranger:
>
> This water pump is in working condition, but the pump needs to be primed in order for the water to come out. Under the white rock, I buried a jar of water, out of the sun. There's enough water in the jar to prime the pump, but not if you drink any first. When you are finished, please fill the jar and put it back as you found it for the next stranger who comes this way.

Just like this hiker, sometimes you have to be willing to pour in everything you have before you can see God's increase flowing in your life. You have to be willing to trust that you can tap into His deep, abundant supply. I encourage you to give God what you have in your hands today, and as you stay faithful to do your part, God will do His part. It takes faith and courage to "prime your pump," but remember, God has already given you what you need to take the first step. When you put action behind your faith, He will pour wisdom, strength, and creativity into you and help you accomplish the dreams and desires He has placed in your heart. He will bring out talents you didn't even know you had. He will give you greater opportunities than you ever dreamed. There is so much untapped talent and potential on the inside of you—gifts, creativity, ideas. Don't let those treasures lie dormant—like that water in the well—instead, be willing to take what you have and prime the pump of faith in your life.

Today, I encourage you to take a step of faith and use what you have. If you have a desire in your heart to teach or minister, start wherever you can, either with a small Bible study or with the children's ministry at your church. You may say, "Oh, I'm made for more than teaching children." Maybe so, but if you'll be faithful with little and do your best, you're sowing a seed. You're giving God something to multiply, and at the right time He'll open up bigger and better doors. Pour in what you have first—prime the pump—because when you tap into the flow of God's blessing, it cannot be contained!

Scripture Reading: 1 Peter 4:8–11

⌘ PRAYER FOR TODAY ⌘

Father in heaven, thank You for filling me and equipping me with everything I need to be successful in this life. I choose to pour in what I have, knowing that I will tap into the flow of Your blessings. Show me Your ways, that I may walk with You and honor You all the days of my life. In Jesus' Name. Amen.

Set the Blessing in Motion

I will make My covenant (solemn pledge) between
Me and you and will multiply you exceedingly.
Genesis 17:2 (AMP)

We serve a God of multiplication! It doesn't matter what your need is today, God already has a plan to increase you and multiply you exceedingly. He wants to meet your needs and pour out His blessing upon you. However, we can't just sit around doing nothing, waiting for God's abundant blessing. God has set up a system in His Word, and when you follow that system, it sets the blessing in motion and opens the door for Him to move on your behalf.

One way to set the blessing into motion is by using the gifts and talents that He has given you to impart good things into the lives of others. Scripture says that when you give, it shall come back to you in greater measure. You can give of your finances and resources but you can also give of yourself to help others grow.

When our son, Jonathan, was just a little boy, he loved attending children's church, and it was because of Mr. Ed. No, we didn't have a talking horse at the church. Mr. Ed was one of the volunteers—a talented, professional artist who used the gifts that God gave him in whatever way he could. He just loved blessing others, so he would draw Bible characters and use stories to help teach the scriptures to children in a fun, relevant way. His drawings were so good and so effective that Jonathan often asked if he could take them home. Mr. Ed had a profound impact on our son and the other children he taught, and we are so grateful. Even though he was amazingly talented, he never once gave the impression that teaching children was beneath him. He gave those kids his very best, and God multiplied his influence exceedingly. When you give what you have in your hand, no matter how small you think it is, God can bless it and multiply it and use it in ways you never imagined.

One time Jesus was preaching to a large crowd on the side of a hill. People traveled a long way to hear Him teach, and they were starting to get hungry. Of course, there wasn't a McDonald's or Domino's Pizza delivery anywhere, so the disciples urged Jesus to send the crowds away so they could travel back home and find food before it got dark. But Jesus said, "I'm not going to turn them away; I'm going to feed them." Then He used the lunch of a small boy— two fish and five dinner rolls—and multiplied it and fed thousands of people that day.

Sometimes what you have seems small. It may feel like you are trying to feed a multitude with five loaves and two fish, but don't limit God the way the disciples did. Nothing is too small in His eyes. His resources are not limited to what you have or what you can see. God is the source of all things, and His supply is limitless. Give Him what you have in your hands and allow Him to multiply it. It doesn't matter what you need today, God can use whatever you have and multiply it to meet your need.

One time in the Old Testament, God multiplied the sound of four men's footsteps and caused them to sound like a mighty army. These four were marching into the enemy's camp, and when their enemies heard them coming, they took off running! Thousands of people, thousands of troops running for their lives, thinking they were being attacked by a massive army, when in fact it was just four people. That's because when you step out in faith, God can make you seem bigger than you really are. He can make you look more powerful, and He can send your enemies running! He knows how to multiply your influence, your strength, and your talent. He can multiply your income or resources. You don't have to figure it all out; you just have to give Him what you have in your hand. Take a step of faith today and use what you have. Set the blessing into motion and believe that with God all things are possible.

Scripture Reading: Deuteronomy 28:1–8

PRAYER FOR TODAY

Father God, today I commit to You everything I have in my hands. I give You my time, talent, and resources to use for Your glory. Thank You for multiplying me and making me more effective in this life. Direct my steps and keep me close to You as I stand in faith for the good things You have in store for me. In Jesus' Name. Amen.

Jump Right In!

*Be careful how you live. Don't live like fools,
but like those who are wise. Make the most of
every opportunity in these evil days.*
Ephesians 5:15–16 (NLT)

When you woke up this morning, God gave you a gift called "today" wrapped in a twenty-four-hour period of time. We must always remember how precious this gift is, because we can never get back the time that has gone by. In fact, your time is the most valuable commodity in life that you have. It's more valuable than money, because you can make more money, but you can't make more time.

Scripture tells us to make the most of our time and every opportunity God has given us. That means we have to be careful how we live and how we approach our days. We can't live this day unfocused, unhappy, negative, or defeated, because God has entrusted us with an assignment and has deposited precious gifts and talents on the inside of each of us. You are a person of destiny, and you have a purpose to live out. The more you use your God-given potential, the more fulfilled and happy you will be. You have to look for those doors of opportunity and be ready to move forward to what God has for you. It's not always easy to step through a door of opportunity. Everyone has things that come against them—fear, distractions, things that steal your time—but sometimes when an opportunity from God comes, we have to be bold and just go for it! We can't waste precious time going needlessly back and forth.

It's like getting into a cold swimming pool on a warm day. You can walk over to the edge and stick your toe in first to check the temperature. Maybe you splash your hand in the water, but that doesn't really help you get used to the temperature. In fact, going in slowly sometimes makes the whole process a bigger deal than it needs to be. It prolongs the inevitable, because it doesn't matter how slowly you try to get in, the water is still going to feel cold to each new body part that hits the water. You can spend twenty minutes trying to get in the pool that way, but it's a whole lot easier if you just jump right in! It only takes a second for your body to adjust to the temperature so you can enjoy your swim that much sooner.

The same is true in life. When an opportunity shows up, and you know it is right for you, don't let fear hold you back. Don't give yourself time to reason it all out, because you can easily talk yourself right out of a God-given opportunity! You can come up with every excuse in the book to stay right where you are, where it's comfortable. Of course that doesn't mean that you should just jump into every opportunity, just like you wouldn't just jump into every pool you see. No, it has to be the right time and the right conditions, but when you know it's right, go for it! Don't waste precious and valuable time. Remember, if God gives you the opportunity, He has already given you the ability to accomplish it.

When I first began speaking at Lakewood, I didn't give myself time to reason it all out in my mind, because I knew I would talk myself out of it. Instead of thinking about all the reasons I couldn't do it, I started thinking about all the reasons I *could* do it. I encouraged myself and allowed the Word of God to empower me. And yes, I was scared! But I knew that God wanted me to step into my position and begin encouraging people. So I took a step of faith, and He was right there with me. I dove right in, and the more I did it, the easier it became. I pressed through my feelings and gained victory, and that is exactly what God wants for you. He wants you to overcome your fear so you can do what He has called you to do.

Let me encourage you: don't shrink back and hide your talent, and don't let excuses keep you from God's best. He wants you to live a fulfilled and rewarding life. He wants you to be refreshed and make the most of every opportunity He's given you. Be a faithful steward of your time, and don't let worry or fear hold you back. You are equipped, you are able, you are not alone. The water is just right, so c'mon and jump right in!

Scripture Reading: Hebrews 12:1–3

PRAYER FOR TODAY

Father in heaven, thank You for the gift of today. I choose to be a faithful steward of the time You've given me by not allowing fear, dread, or procrastination to hold me back. Thank You for Your Word that empowers me and strengthens me to do what You've called me to. In Jesus' Name. Amen.

Chapter Six

Recovering
Lost Opportunities

He'll Get You Back on Track

"I know the plans I have for you," declares the LORD, "plans to prosper you and not to harm you, plans to give you hope and a future."
Jeremiah 29:11 (NIV)

When I look back over my life, I can see where I've missed out on some God-given opportunities. Maybe you could say the same thing. If so, I want to encourage you: Don't live in regret. Don't let lost opportunities make you feel disappointed and discouraged. Know that God is bigger than your lost opportunities and He can still get you to where you need to be in life.

Have you ever used one of those GPS devices in your car? You set the location to where you want to go, and the GPS calculates the best route. You can be driving along and get distracted and completely miss the street where the GPS instructed you to turn, but that doesn't mean you'll never reach your destination. That GPS will instantly recalculate the route based on your present location.

God works in a similar way. He is constantly giving us direction, speaking to our hearts, leading us by peace in our spirits; but even when we miss His instructions—and we all do from time to time—He will recalculate our route and get us back where we need to be. But we'll never reach our destination if we are constantly trying to look back over our shoulders to see where we should have turned in the first place. We have to forget about what we've missed so we can focus on what lies ahead.

I love what the apostle Paul said in Philippians, "This one thing I do: Forgetting what is behind I press forward to what is ahead." Paul was saying in essence, "*This one thing* I'm going to focus on more than anything else." "*This one thing* is the most important key to living the life of victory." "*This one thing* will carry me to my destiny." *This one thing*—forgetting the past and looking forward. Like Paul, we have to aggressively turn our thoughts away from where we've been, away from our mistakes, away from our "missed turns," and turn our thoughts forward, in the direction we are headed. We have to keep looking for the new opportunities in our paths and shake off regret and disappointments. This is a new day, and God wants to do a new thing in your life.

Today, it doesn't matter if you've made some wrong choices or if you've gotten off track; God knows right where you are, and He has a new route ready for you. He wants to restore those opportunities that once seemed lost forever. It may not always be the way you thought, but if you'll stay open, He'll get you back on track and bless you beyond your wildest dreams.

Scripture Reading: Isaiah 45:2–7

PRAYER FOR TODAY

Heavenly Father, thank You for guiding and directing my every step. I trust that You hold my future securely in Your hand. I choose to release the past and forget past mistakes or "wrong turns" and focus my attention on You, the author and finisher of my faith. In Jesus' Name. Amen.

The God of the Impossible

Nothing is impossible with God.
Luke 1:37 (NIV)

Are you facing a situation in your life that seems impossible—something in your relationships, finances, or maybe in your physical body? Anytime you don't know what to do or how to do it, remember this: God does. He is not confined to the resources of this earthly realm. He is the God of the impossible! When you don't see any options in the natural, remember, there's always an option you may not be able to see. There's always another way that I've mentioned before called the *God option.*

In the book of Genesis, God promised Abraham and Sarah that they would have a son and that all the generations of the earth would be blessed through him. In the natural, this looked impossible because Sarah was ninety and Abraham was older than that. They could have easily looked at their situation and decided, "There is just no way." But, even though they couldn't see a way in the natural, they chose to put their faith and trust in God. They chose to meditate on God and consider what He could do beyond their earthly limitations. Hebrews 11 tells us that their faith opened the door for God to bring to pass what He had promised in their lives. When they considered God, He did the impossible: He strengthened their mortal bodies so they could conceive a child even beyond Sarah's childbearing years.

Remember this: when things look impossible in your life, there is more happening than what you can see. The God of the impossible is working behind the scenes. Even when your hands are tied, His hands are never tied. When it looks like there is nothing in your bank account, God has an unlimited supply. He promises to meet every single one of your needs according to His riches in glory. When a relationship seems broken beyond repair, God is the God of restoration. He can soften and mend people's hearts. When you need an opportunity to open up and you can't see a way, don't give up, because God can make a way. He knows how to get you to the right place at the right time. He can cause the right people to have favor on you and bring you the right connections. He is always working behind the scenes for your good.

Just like Abraham and Sarah did, broaden your thinking and keep an attitude of expectancy. Put actions behind your faith and do everything you know to do in the natural. Press past what your mind is telling you and consider the God option. Keep your heart and mind focused on Him because He is ready, willing, and able to do the impossible in your life!

Scripture Reading: Genesis 17

PRAYER FOR TODAY

Heavenly Father, I come to You today, rejoicing that You are the God of the impossible! I choose to focus my heart and mind on You, knowing that You will make a way where there seems to be no way. Thank You for Your faithfulness. Thank You for Your peace. Thank You for equipping me with everything I need to accomplish the dreams and desires You've placed inside of me. I lift my eyes to You with faith and expectancy! In Jesus' Name. Amen.

He Brings Back Opportunities

*I am with you and will watch over you wherever
you go, and I will bring you back to this land.
I will not leave you until I have done
what I have promised you.*
Genesis 28:15 (NIV)

One Christmas several years before Joel and I took leadership of Lakewood Church, I had a desire in my heart to share God's love in a special way with the needy in our community. I began thinking about all the women in shelters and homes around the city and wanted to do a little something to help brighten their holiday season and let them know they were valuable and not forgotten. The idea came to me to make some Christmas baskets filled with perfume and toiletries. I was so overjoyed at the thought and couldn't wait to get started! I found the phone number of a nearby shelter so I could call and get an idea of what the women needed most and how many baskets I should make. I dialed the number, and when a sweet-sounding lady answered, I immediately began telling her what I wanted to do and how I had hoped to make the women at the shelter feel special. However, rather than getting excited with me and giving me the information I needed, the woman began to grill me with questions. She said, "This is a private facility and the women need to remain anonymous." Then she asked, "Have you been abused? Do you know somebody who has been abused? Do you need help, are you looking for help?"

"No," I said. "I just want to brighten the holiday for the women." She went on and on as though she hadn't even heard me, thinking that I was trying to disguise an abuse that I had suffered. Finally I ended the conversation and hung up the phone feeling frustrated because my idea was seemingly being blocked. I thought to myself, *I'll call back tomorrow and speak with someone else.* But, as life goes sometimes, I became busy with family and holiday projects. Before I knew it, the Christmas season had passed and I had missed that opportunity.

A few weeks later as I was praying, I remembered those Christmas baskets and the opportunity that I had allowed to slip away. I shared my heart with God and explained that I had lost my determination and felt like I let those women down somehow. I asked Him to present another opportunity to me, and I promised that this time I would see it through no matter what.

Several months went by and then, out of the blue, I received a telephone call from The Bridge, a women's shelter in Houston similar to the one that I had contacted. A woman named Jackie was on the other end of the phone line. "Hi, Victoria, I'm the director of The Bridge," she told me, "and I attend Lakewood Church. I want to invite you to speak at my Women of Distinction Awards program, a benefit for the women's shelter." She told me all about the event and that there would be city leaders, business leaders, and others in attendance. Clearly she was so happy and proud of this event and how it would raise so much money to help the women in the shelter. As she was speaking, I remembered those Christmas baskets and the prayer I had prayed. I was so honored by her request and immediately said, "Yes!" At the time, I didn't have a lot of experience speaking in front of large audiences and when I hung up the phone, I thought, *Oh God, those Christmas baskets would have been so much easier! Couldn't I have just started there?* I had butterflies in my stomach just thinking about it! But even though I was nervous, I felt that this was the opportunity I had prayed and asked God for.

I worked so hard to prepare my presentation and I rehearsed over and over in my mind what I would say. When the time came to speak, I was really nervous, but afterward, I felt that I had done my best. I was so honored to be a part of helping the women in such a unique way. Several people approached me, saying they were so inspired by my words. But what struck me the most was that later on, a professional athlete and his wife were so moved by my presentation that they made a large donation to the shelter. That donation helped those women way more than my Christmas baskets ever could!

It took faith, stretching, and hard work but it was marvelous to see how God brought back an opportunity that I had missed earlier. He used me to bless those women way beyond what I could have ever imagined, and I know He can do something similar for you.

Maybe you're thinking of an opportunity you missed along life's road. For one reason or another, we've all allowed opportunities to slip through our fingers. But we can't afford to get trapped in regret, or we'll miss the opportunities God has for our future. Instead, why don't you ask God to bring back those missed opportunities? Be bold today and dare to believe His promises. He is a rewarder and He is a restorer and He can bring back around every desire, every dream, and every opportunity.

Scripture Reading: Joel 2:18–27

 PRAYER FOR TODAY

Heavenly Father, thank You for Your healing power and restoration in my life. I know that You are good and You desire to bring back

every opportunity that I may have missed in my past. Today, I lay down guilt and condemnation and lift up my eyes to You, the Author and Finisher of my faith. Thank You for filling my heart with expectation as I look for the new opportunities You have for me. In Jesus' Name. Amen.

Be Open to a New Way

See, I am doing a new thing! Now it
springs up; do you not perceive it?
Isaiah 43:19 (NIV)

Sometimes, when we are believing and expecting something specific from God, we have to be open to it happening in a way we didn't imagine. We have to trust in God's goodness, knowing that His ways are so much higher and better than our own. He always has your best interest at heart, he always has good things in store for you, but the plan He has for you may be different from what you originally thought. The destination may be the same, but the route to get there may be different. In order to receive all the blessings God has for us, we need to stay open and look for the new ways God wants to work in our lives.

Joel's sister, Lisa, and her husband, Kevin, tried for years to have children. Lisa went through many fertility treatments and several surgeries, but still was not able to conceive. Finally the doctor told them there was nothing more he could do; they weren't going to be able to have children. Lisa and Kevin were devastated. It looked as if their dreams had died, but God still had a plan and He was working behind the scenes on their behalf. One day out of the blue,

Lisa received a phone call from Nancy Alcorn of Mercy Ministries, a home for at-risk young women based in Nashville.

"Lisa, I normally wouldn't do this," Nancy said, "but we have a young woman who is about to give birth to twin girls, and we were wondering if you and Kevin might be interested in adopting them?"

At the time, Lisa and Kevin had not yet considered adoption since they were still hoping to have children naturally, but suddenly Lisa's interest was piqued.

"There's only one problem," Nancy said. "It appears that you and Kevin have most of the qualifications that the birth mother is looking for the adoptive parents to have, but she also has a stipulation that her babies be placed in a family with twins in their background."

What Nancy didn't know is that Kevin has a twin sister. As soon as Lisa heard that, her heart leapt and confirmed that this was a "God opportunity." A few months later, Lisa and Kevin adopted those twin baby girls, and then three years later, they adopted another "Mercy" baby boy.

God gave Kevin and Lisa three beautiful children even though it happened differently from what they first expected. They kept their hearts open for what God wanted to do in their lives, and He gave them another opportunity to be the parents they desired to be. They could have just as easily given up and closed their minds, but they didn't. They remained open, and God brought back that opportunity in a different way. Lisa will tell you, "These children came straight from my heart. I couldn't have had better children!"

Be encouraged because even if things haven't gone your way in the past and you think your dreams have died, remember God has new opportunities ahead. I believe God is saying today, "I can restore the years that you've lost. Will you allow me to do a new thing in your life?"

Remember, God is good and you can trust Him. He wants the rest of your life to be the best of your life! Stay open to Him and keep an attitude of faith and expectancy because He is working on your behalf to fulfill every desire of your heart.

Scripture Reading: Isaiah 55:8–13

PRAYER FOR TODAY

Dear God, today I come humbly to You, giving You all that I am. I release every hurt, every disappointment, every broken dream to You. I trust that You are working behind the scenes on my behalf and that You will fulfill every desire that You've placed in my heart. I love You and bless You today. In Jesus' Name. Amen.

Dream Another Dream

*Very truly I tell you, unless a kernel of wheat falls
to the ground and dies, it remains only a single
seed. But if it dies, it produces many seeds.*

John 12:24 (NIV)

We've all had losses in life or things that seemed to just slip
through our fingers: opportunities, relationships, connections, and even dreams. Sometimes, you might feel robbed or
cheated when this happens. You might be tempted to start getting
down on yourself, thinking, *If only . . .* , or looking for what you
could have done differently. But instead of considering those things
as lost, why don't you consider them to be seeds that will yield a
harvest in your future? When you bury a seed, it's not gone forever;
no, you are actually unlocking its full potential. Even though you
can't see it, the life inside the seed is at work in the dark, fertile soil.
You may not know when that seed is going to produce a harvest,
but have faith because at the right time, it will.

A few years ago, I received a letter from a woman named Micki
McHay whose husband had recently passed away. She was so distraught and brokenhearted. She described how she couldn't see a
way to make it through such a painful experience. She began to
pray and ask God to help her. One night she was reading Joel's

book and came across the statement, "When one dream dies, dream another dream."

Those words touched her heart so deeply. She remembered how she had started writing a children's book many years before that she had never finished. At that moment, faith was reignited in her heart. She felt God was opening another door in her life. She made the decision that she was going to pick up where she left off and pursue her dream. She found an illustrator and a publisher, and it wasn't long before she released *The Ugly Snowflake*, a delightful children's book about a little snowflake that discovered her true, unique beauty.

The letter she sent me was accompanied by an autographed copy of her book, which my young daughter would ask me to read to her over and over again. Not only did God rebirth a dream in Micki McHay's heart, but He is using it to bless and encourage children everywhere.

Maybe you've gone through a loss and it looks like a dream has died, but if you'll search your heart, and dare to dream another dream, you can see great days up ahead! Consider that loss a seed. Believe that its roots are growing strong and soon it will begin to flourish and produce fruit. You may not be able to see it happening, it may seem dark, but trust that the seed is growing. No matter what has happened in your past, don't give up! Dare to dream another dream because God has great things in store for your future.

Scripture Reading: Isaiah 40:26–31

PRAYER FOR TODAY

Heavenly Father, thank You for every dream and desire You've placed in my heart. Today, I surrender every disappointment, every question, every hurt, and every difficulty to You. I thank You that no experience in my life is lost, but You are turning it around and using it for good in my future. Thank You for filling me with Your peace as I keep my heart and mind stayed on You. In Jesus' Name. Amen.

He Restores Relationships

The LORD says, "I will give you back what you lost . . ."
Joel 2:25 (NLT)

When people look back over their lives, most times their greatest regrets involve opportunities missed in relationships or with loved ones. But God doesn't want us to live one single minute in regret. He wants to restore the moments, days, or years that have been lost or stolen. In the blink of an eye, He can restore relationships and strengthen those connections moving forward.

One day Joel and I were sitting together on the sofa looking at pictures of our children when they were young and just enjoying the memories. We came across some photos of Alexandra when she was in her "little princess" stage and I said to Joel, "Aren't these pictures darling? Remember when we had that princess birthday party, and everything was pink?"

Joel's face looked puzzled. "You know, Victoria, I don't really remember that. I know I must have been there, but I don't have a strong memory of that time."

As Joel and I talked about it, we realized that he didn't have the same memories of Alexandra's early childhood as he did of Jonathan's. You see, Alexandra was a newborn when Joel's father passed away. We were thrust into leading Lakewood Church, and we were both just doing our best to stay above water. Overnight, Joel's responsibilities increased one hundredfold. Everyone was vying for his time and he was being pulled in every direction. The church was growing at an astonishing rate and the pressure on him was enormous. On top of all that, he was suddenly preaching on TV to millions of people, all of whom had come to expect a masterpiece each week. For the first three years of his ministry, Joel's mind was consumed by the awesome responsibility that landed in his lap. No wonder Joel had a hard time remembering those early years in Alexandra's life.

After we talked for a few minutes, Joel and I prayed that God would make up those years to him. Today, I can tell you that Joel and Alexandra are as close as any father and daughter can be. Alexandra loves to do everything with her daddy. They play outside together and even go to the mall together. Alexandra is for sure her daddy's girl. Joel has always made every effort to be the best dad he could be to both of our children, and I believe God crowned his efforts with success and strengthened their bond even though those early years were such a whirlwind.

Maybe something similar has happened to you and you feel like you weren't as good a parent or friend as you should have been. Perhaps you were busy just trying to keep your head above water, and consequently, your relationships suffered. You may be tempted to feel guilty and think, *If I had just spent more time with them, and made them a higher priority.* However, fretting over missed opportunities won't make a difference, but asking God to give you another chance will. Pray and ask Him to show you how to reach out to that person and make up for lost time. Be open for a new way to connect with the people you love because when you are open and look for creative ways to communicate with the people in your life, God will help you. You may have missed some good chances, but ultimately, God's goal is to restore your relationships. Trust Him because He will make up the difference and, just like with Joel and Alexandra, He'll make things better than you ever thought possible!

Scripture Reading: Ephesians 3:14–21

⁓ PRAYER FOR TODAY ⁓

Heavenly Father, thank You for Your truth which is life and freedom to my soul. Today, I give you my relationships. I give You my lost opportunities. I ask that You restore the years and moments that have been stolen. Strengthen my connections with the people I love and give me creative ways to show my love. In Jesus' Name. Amen.

Double for Your Trouble

Because you got a double dose of trouble and more than your share of contempt, your inheritance in the land will be doubled and your joy go on forever.
Isaiah 61:7 (MSG)

When this scripture in Isaiah 61 was written, God's people were going through a very difficult time. They were being held captive against their will and mistreated by other nations. God sent this word to encourage them and give them hope for their future. To make a really long story short, in the end God was faithful to His Word. He restored a double inheritance to His people and filled them with everlasting joy.

Maybe your circumstances aren't quite like what they were going through, but every person experiences disappointments, setbacks, and things that don't seem to make sense. Even when you are doing all the right things, sometimes the wrong thing happens anyway. It's easy to get discouraged and think, *Why did this happen to me? Why did my loved one not make it? Why did this person treat me wrong? Why did I get laid off?* I had a man tell me how he lost his job after many years with his former company. He just didn't understand it. He said, "I gave them my best. I was always on time, I was loyal—it's just not fair." But we have to understand that even when life is not fair, God is always fair. He is always with us in our darkest hour, working behind the scenes to deliver us and restore hope for our future. That disappointment is not the end; your life doesn't stop because of a setback. No, God has an amazing future in store for you if you'll take Him by the hand and let Him lead you to a place of safety and rest.

Just like God's Word brought encouragement to the Israelites so many years ago, let this word bring encouragement to you, because God is working on your behalf and he wants to give you double for your trouble! You may be thinking you've wasted years of your life in the wrong career or associating with the wrong people, but God is saying, "I can restore those years." You may think that it's been too long, you've been through too much, and you're never going to see those new seasons of increase. But God can make up for that lost time. Why don't you be bold and ask Him to give you back every opportunity that you've missed? He may not always do it in the way you are expecting, but open your heart and mind to the possibilities. Be ready to embrace the opportunities God will bring across your path. When God brings restoration, He's not just going to repay you for every wrong done, He's going to go above and beyond and make things even better than they were before.

If you are facing challenges today or going through a time of adversity, remember, it's always darkest just before the dawn appears. Your days are destined to shine brighter because God is faithful. Trust that He is working behind the scenes on your behalf and for your good! As you stay in faith and are obedient to His Word, you'll receive double for your trouble and see every one of His promises come to pass!

Scripture Reading: Revelation 21:1–7

⚬══════⚬ PRAYER FOR TODAY ⚬══════⚬

Father God, thank You for Your Word which lights my path and guides my steps. I choose to put my trust and hope in You today, knowing that You are always with me, even in my darkest hour. Thank You for bringing restoration into my life as I keep my heart and mind stayed on You. In Jesus' Name. Amen.

Chapter Seven

Overcoming Offenses

When Offense Comes

He who covers and forgives an offense seeks love . . .
Proverbs 17:9 (AMP)

My entire life, my family has been in the jewelry business. I practically grew up in the jewelry store, helping my mother and waiting on customers from the time I was in elementary school. Over the years, I've learned quite a bit about gemstones and precious metals, but the story of how a pearl is formed has always fascinated me most.

Most people know that a pearl comes from an oyster. But not every oyster has a pearl, and it isn't just random chance when an oyster does have one. In fact, that little oyster has to do a lot of work and endure quite a bit of hardship in order to make a pearl. The most amazing part of the process is that the oyster's goal isn't even to make a pearl; the oyster's goal is to protect itself from a foreign substance—an offending irritant.

A pearl is formed when a single grain of sand or a tiny foreign particle is lodged inside an oyster. If left alone, that tiny particle will cause damage to the lining of the tender mollusk. The particle is an irritant, which causes the oyster to produce a lacquer-like substance called nacre. The oyster secretes the nacre over that irritant as a way of protecting itself. It constantly works to shield itself from the irritant. Those smooth layers of nacre coat the sand granule, eventually sealing off the irritation and forming a gorgeous pearl.

Now I'm sure you've had a few irritants in your days. Everyone has. If they aren't handled properly, those irritants can easily become offenses that will lodge in your heart and do some serious damage, keeping you from God's best. But if we follow the example of the oyster, and refuse to allow that irritant to embed in us, then God can make a beautiful pearl in our lives.

Now, the oyster doesn't waste any time dealing with that irritant. It doesn't say, "Oh, I'm just too tired to deal with that. I have too many other things going on. I'll deal with it later." No, it instantly begins to work to protect itself. Pushing out the offending irritant is automatic to the oyster, and we should become so skilled at pushing out offenses that it becomes automatic to us. Throughout life, unfair things will happen. People will let you down, they'll say things that hurt you, and they won't always treat you the way you think they should. If you meditate on the disappointment, it allows the offense to take root in your heart. Before long, bitterness enters the scene and steals your joy and enthusiasm for life. The way to insulate yourself from offense and keep your heart pure is to release the hurt to God and allow Him to produce the priceless pearl your life is meant to be. Just like that oyster covers that irritant with nacre, so we must cover offenses with love and grace in order to protect our hearts from being damaged. Doing so is not always easy and it takes some work, but the result is worth it. Start by simply making the choice to forgive and to declare God's Word over your circumstance and over that person who hurt you. Although that may not be easy, scripture tells us to bless those who curse us and pray for those who spitefully use us. Every time you declare, "I forgive that person and I bless them in Jesus' name" it's like covering that offense with a beautiful layer of love.

Why don't you take a few minutes right now and ask the Lord to search your heart for any "grains of sand" that have been lodged in your heart? Ask Him to help you to forgive and remove that destructive irritant. Don't waste another precious moment in life holding on to an offense because it will only damage you. Release it to Him because you are worth it and your future is worth it. Push out the irritants and let Him turn them into beautiful, precious pearls of victory in your life.

Scripture Reading: Luke 6:27–31

PRAYER FOR TODAY

Father God, thank You for loving me and setting me free from all bitterness and offense. Search my heart and reveal to me anything that is not pleasing to You. Help me, by Your Spirit, to cover any offenses with love. I choose forgiveness today and bless those who have hurt me. Be glorified in my life, today. In Jesus' name. Amen.

Don't Let the World Strip You of Your Robe

I delight greatly in the LORD; my soul rejoices in my God. For He has clothed me with garments of salvation and arrayed me in a robe of His righteousness.

Isaiah 61:10 (NIV)

One of my favorite stories in the Bible is the story of Jacob's son, Joseph. Joseph was a young boy dearly loved by His father. His father distinguished him from his eleven brothers with a beautiful, luxurious coat of many colors, a richly ornamented robe. That coat represented many things; it set Joseph apart as special and symbolized the favor and affection of his father. It also represented God's mantle and anointing on his life. Overall, that beautiful coat displayed his identity. As you might imagine, Joseph's brothers were jealous of that coat and all that it represented. They didn't like him very much to begin with so this, of course, didn't help the situation. In fact, they were so jealous and angry that they plotted to kill him. One day, they found their opportunity and ambushed him, stripped him of his coat, and threw him into a well. Thankfully, one of the brothers pleaded with the others to sell Joseph into slavery rather than kill him, and they all finally agreed.

I find it interesting, though, that the first thing they did was strip him of his coat. I believe they were really trying to strip him of his identity, favor, and anointing in order to level the playing field, so to speak.

Soon after, Joseph was taken to Egypt and sold to Potipher, a high-ranking official. Joseph used his gifts and talents and found great favor. Even though he was stripped of his coat from his earthly father, he wasn't going to let anyone strip him of his robe of righteousness from his Heavenly Father! The Bible says he excelled in Potipher's house and that Potipher's wife took notice of him. She tried to trick him and seduce him, but Joseph stood strong. When she approached him begging him to go to bed with her, he turned around and took off running. And you know what she did? The Bible says she grabbed his cloak as he ran out the door! She tried to steal his robe of righteousness, and when she couldn't have that, she took the cloak off his back.

Now, that's not the end of the story. Even though Joseph was knocked down many times, He rose up in great victory. God blessed him beyond his wildest dreams. His journey is a powerful reminder that all throughout life, the enemy of our souls will try to strip us of our identity, favor, and righteousness given to us through the precious blood of Jesus. We have to stay on guard and be aware of all the subtle ways this can happen.

For example, I have a friend who is a beautiful, talented, vibrant woman. She has an upbeat personality, always positive and passionate. But not everyone embraces her optimistic attitude. One day at work, as she entered the boardroom for an early-morning meeting, she overheard a few of her coworkers talking about her. They said, "She is just so over-the-top all the time. Sometimes I want to say to her, 'Are you for real?' Oh, no. Here she comes. I just don't know if I can take her perkiness this morning."

My friend didn't say anything at the time, but those words really wounded her heart. It was as if someone tried to snatch her gorgeous "coat" away from her. Instead of going into that meeting with her positive attitude and sparkling personality, she quietly took her seat and remained withdrawn. She began doubting herself and tried to adjust her personality to counteract the words she had overheard earlier.

Shortly after, she joined me and a group of friends for lunch. I noticed right away that she seemed different, so I asked her what was wrong. After a moment of hesitation, she told us what had happened. She said she was going to tone down her personality so she would be more accepted by the other women in the office. After hearing that, I said, "Are you kidding me? You are one of the brightest, most outgoing, wonderful women I know! Your personality is great and you can use it to influence a lot of people for good. Don't change who you are simply because your coworkers can't appreciate your gifts!"

Immediately my friend realized that she was letting her coworkers' disapproval strip her of her God-given identity. She had allowed it to steal her joy and to negatively affect her self-esteem. Right there, she made the choice to proudly wear her "coat" because her heavenly Father made it just for her!

Do you ever find that you try to adjust who you are in order to be accepted by others? You may not be like everyone else, but that's okay. Be who God made you to be and do not be defined by the opinions of other people. You may get knocked down sometimes, but just like Joseph, you will rise again! Don't let the world strip you of your robe; you are created in the image of Almighty God, and He gave you the gifts and personality you have for a purpose. Keep doing what you know is right in the eyes of God, and He'll pour out His favor on you in ways you never imagined!

Scripture Reading: Genesis 37

⌒⌒⌒ PRAYER FOR TODAY ⌒⌒⌒

Father God, thank You for loving me and creating me with unique gifts, talents, and abilities. Thank You for identifying me as your own with a royal robe of righteousness. I stand today, confident in You because You have anointed and equipped me for every good work. In Jesus' Name. Amen.

Let It Bounce Right off of You

A person's wisdom yields patience;
it is to one's glory to overlook an offense.
Proverbs 19:11 (NIV)

My daughter Alexandra loves gymnastics. She loves to do back bends, cartwheels, twists, and turns. She is always saying, "Mommy, watch this," as she tries something new. I remember a few years ago when she began learning how to do one-handed cartwheels; she spent a day or two practicing them in the living room and then I noticed that she began doing something else. I asked her how her cartwheel was coming along and if she would do one for me. To my complete surprise, she declined; in fact, I could tell that my request bothered her. I asked her why she didn't want to do one. "Mom," she said hesitantly, "Curtis told me I wasn't good at it, and he made fun of me. So I am going to learn to do a roundabout instead." Curtis was one of the boys in her class at school, and at the moment, I was not too happy with him!

I thought for a moment and then asked, "Oh! Is Curtis a cartwheel expert?"

She looked at me slightly perplexed and then answered, "No!"

"Perhaps he is an Olympic gymnast?" I asked.

"No!" she said. I could tell she was beginning to understand my point.

"Well then, he must surely be a cartwheel expert of some kind."

By now a smile was on her face. "Mom, you know he is not an expert in cartwheels!"

"Well then, do you believe you are not good at cartwheels just because Curtis told you so?" I asked.

Alexandra completely understood what I was telling her. We talked a little bit more about it and then she did half a dozen cartwheels for me, and I kissed her brightened little face. As I turned to go into the kitchen, I heard her chanting that old kids' rhyme: "I'm rubber and you're glue, whatever you say, bounces off me and sticks to you!"

I laughed at her sweet, innocent perspective, and then I thought, *There's a lot of truth to that old rhyme.* If we as adults could get that into our hearts, it would serve us well! Certainly, we should always consider the constructive opinions of the people we respect, but we should never let anyone's words alter our personality or deter us from using our gifts and talents. That's why the scripture tells us to overlook offense. It's easy to allow cutting remarks to revolve over and over in our minds. We may try to make sense of it all or convince ourselves that it's not true, but we have to stay on the offensive and not allow those words to sink into our hearts. The criticism of others isn't necessarily true. Ephesians tells us that people aren't our enemies, anyway. Our battle is not against flesh and blood; that's why we have to take captive every thought and instead choose to meditate on what God says about us. His Word is true and lasts forever. Don't ever let the words of others define you; instead, insulate the offense and let it bounce right off of you!

Scripture Reading: Ephesians 6:10–20

⌘⌘⌘ PRAYER FOR TODAY ⌘⌘⌘

Father God, thank You for the gifts, talents, and abilities you've placed inside of me. Thank You for approving me and accepting me. I choose to let go of the criticism of others and take hold of Your Word which is truth that sets me free. Thank You for working in my heart today and giving me the discernment to make right choices in this life. In Jesus' Name. Amen.

Make Amends Quickly

Blessed are the peacemakers,
for they will be called children of God.
Matthew 5:9 (NIV)

Many people think that peace is about *not* arguing or about simply being quiet, but really it's about much more than that. Biblical peace is a powerful spiritual position. One of the root definitions in the original Greek means "to set at one again." In other words, when you are joined as one with Almighty God in thought, purpose, and deed, you are in a position of peace. When you are thinking His thoughts, speaking His Words, and following His example, you are living a life of peace.

In the same way, when we pursue peace with others, it doesn't mean that we just refrain from arguing with them or that we just stay quiet around them. Peace takes effort. It happens when we make amends quickly and don't allow offense to take root in our hearts. You may not always agree with everyone, but you can still have peace when you agree to disagree and choose to respect each other's differences.

One thing I find interesting about the oyster is when a grain of sand, an offending irritant, makes its way into its shell, that oyster doesn't let much time pass before it begins working to push out

173

that irritant. In fact, it doesn't let the sand linger at all because the oyster knows it will cause so much damage. In the same way for us, if we allow offenses to hang around, they will cause damage that can be nearly impossible to reverse. The results can be devastating.

Two sisters, Shelly and Susan, have been friends of our family for many years. Several years ago, they shared the traumatic experience of their mother going through a prolonged illness and eventually dying. Up until that time, Shelly and Susan had been very close, and at first they rallied together and found comfort in each other—until it came time to deal with their mother's rather modest estate, which consisted of a small house, some furniture, and about $50,000 in life insurance. Their mother's will provided for each of the daughters to receive an equal share.

Shortly after the funeral, Shelly, Susan, and Susan's husband, Tom, were sitting in Shelly's dining room discussing whether they were going to sell the house or rent it out, when Tom blurted out, "You know, Shelly, your mother always loved you the most and it seems that Susan should get the house just to even things out!"

Shelly was floored and hardly knew what to say to Tom, when she noticed that Susan was nodding her head in agreement. "Susan, why are you nodding your head?" she asked. Susan looked at Tom then back at Shelly and began to tell Shelly how she had always felt that way. "You were mom's little princess," she said. "You could do no wrong." Susan then spent the next ten minutes telling Shelly how much she resented her for that. As you might imagine, the conversation quickly became a heated argument filled with accusations and hurtful words. Finally, Susan and Tom stormed out of the house, got into their car, and sped away.

The next afternoon Shelly received a notice from Susan's attorney informing her that Susan was contesting their mother's will. Now Shelly was offended as well, and she became angry at Susan. She picked up the phone and called a friend who referred her to an attorney. A year and a half later, the case was settled. The house was sold to pay attorney's fees and each of the sisters received about $25,000—well short of what they could have received had they not allowed their offenses to devastate their relationship. The saddest part of all is that they have not spoken to each other since that day in Shelly's dining room.

As a family, they were torn apart by lingering offenses. The entire episode could have been avoided had Susan confided in her sister and dealt with her negative feelings years earlier instead of allowing the bitterness and resentment to grow in her heart. That's why it's so important to make amends quickly and pursue peace.

Today, if you are holding on to an offense, let it go. Nothing is worth the damage that offense can do in your relationships and in your own life. Make the choice to pursue peace. Set your heart and mind on things above, things that matter in eternity. Make peace a priority because when you are a peacemaker, God says you are blessed, you are connected to Him, and you are able to move forward in the freedom and victory He has prepared for you.

Scripture Reading: Romans 12:14–21

 PRAYER FOR TODAY

Father God, I humbly come before You inviting You to have Your way in my heart. I choose to be a peacemaker. I choose to align myself with You in thought, word, and deed. Help me to forgive others and overlook offense so I can live in the peace and blessing You have prepared for me. In Jesus' Name. Amen.

Deal with the Little Things

Catch for us the foxes, the little foxes
that ruin the vineyards . . .
Song of Solomon 2:15 (NIV)

Most often, it isn't the major challenges, upsets, or difficulties that affect relationships, but it's the little things, minor irritations, hurtful words, or short answers day in and day out that build and create a wedge. It's the little foxes that ruin the vineyards. We have to be careful to watch our attitudes and responses and make sure that we honor and respect the people we love. We can't allow disrespect to take root in our hearts because it is a seed that when planted can wreak havoc on healthy relationships.

I remember one time early in our marriage, Joel and I were having a disagreement and there was no way that we were going to see eye to eye. My feelings were hurt and I was highly frustrated. Joel, on the other hand, didn't see our disagreement as a big deal and had grown tired of talking about it. So, to end the discussion, he half-heartedly said, "I'm sorry." That was good enough for him and he went about his business. I headed for the other room and when I got behind the closed door, I turned around and stuck out my tongue at him. It seemed innocent enough, and I was just blowing off steam, but even through my frustration, I knew it was disrespectful. After a few minutes of contemplation, I realized that I couldn't allow that disrespect to take root in my heart; I had to deal with it quickly. So I went back into the kitchen to Joel and told him that even though he was wrong, I loved him and respected him. Joel simply smiled and said, "I knew you would come around."

I really believe that if I had allowed that disrespect and frustration to take root in my heart, it wouldn't have taken long for other little offenses to creep in, too. Who knows how that could have affected our relationship? But I'm so thankful I listened to the inner prompting of the Holy Spirit to deal with that disrespect quickly. I chose to uproot that seed of offense and, instead, planted seeds of peace, the harvest I wanted in our future.

Remember, if you start showing disrespect even in small ways, soon it will manifest itself in larger displays that will strain and weaken a good relationship. Choose to uproot any bad seeds you may have sown in the past by making peace and sowing love. If there's someone coming to mind right now, a friend, coworker, or family member, ask God to show you how to deal with that offense and sow a seed of peace. Choose forgiveness because forgiveness sets you free. Deal with the little things quickly and let your relationships blossom into strong, vibrant, lasting connections.

Scripture Reading: Ephesians 4:31–5:4

 PRAYER FOR TODAY

Heavenly Father, I open my heart and mind to You today. I invite You to search me and know my heart. Uproot any negative seeds of disrespect or bitterness that may be keeping me from enjoying my relationships to the fullest. Help me see others the way You see them so I can move forward in peace in every area of my life. In Jesus' Name. Amen.

Letting Go and Moving Forward

Do not seek revenge or bear a grudge against anyone
among your people, but love your neighbor as yourself.
Leviticus 19:18 (NIV)

So often, people hold on to bitterness or resentment, thinking that they are stockpiling ammunition against the person who hurt or offended them, as if one day they'll have the chance to settle the score. Or, perhaps they hold on to all the evidence waiting for their day in "emotional court." However, the truth is, if you don't choose to forgive, the only person being punished is you.

Unforgiveness is like a barrier that actually blocks the door to your heart. You must choose to remove the barrier, open the door of your heart, and extend forgiveness to others. When the door of your heart is open, you can release all the hurt and pain and make room for God's healing. But if that door to your heart is blocked, if forgiveness doesn't come out of you, then God's forgiveness can't flow into you. Matthew 6:15 tells us that if we don't forgive others, God cannot forgive us.

I heard a story about a woman in her mid thirties who had been in an abusive and tumultuous marriage. Her husband was a heavy drinker, had several affairs, and finally abandoned her and their three young children. The woman had a nursing degree, but she hadn't ever worked. Understandably, she had many worries and concerns. It was as if the weight of the world was on her shoulders. On top of that, she was consumed with feelings of betrayal, anger, and hurt. Some nights, she would stay awake imagining confrontations with her former husband. In her mind, she would play over and over all of the offenses and wrongs that he had committed. She wanted so badly to get even.

This was the most difficult time of her life and the only solace she could find was in her faith in God. One night while praying, she realized that if she ever wanted to get her life back, she would have to let go of all of the offenses. God had revealed to her that all the anger and offense was weighing her down and holding her back. It was affecting her outlook on life and creating a wedge in her relationship with her heavenly Father.

One day, she was finally ready to let go of the hurt and offense. To help her do this, she imagined a large assortment of helium-filled balloons in her hand. Each balloon represented an offense, concern, hurt, or worry in her life. Then she pictured herself releasing those balloons one at a time and watching those offenses float away. As she did this, she could almost physically feel each of those offenses, cares, and concerns lifting off of her. As she let go of those cares and concerns, she received a fresh portion of God's strength to face each day. As time passed, she was able to move forward with her life. Today, she is the head nurse at a well-known nonprofit clinic. Her children have all gone into the medical profession—two are doctors and one is a nurse. She found her place of peace as she released those balloons and learned to forgive.

Why don't you release *your* balloons today? Choose to let go of all the offenses and give them to God. You can accomplish so much more without the weight of those burdens dragging you down. God wants you to be happy and free, so keep your heart open to forgiveness and make room for His healing power to restore your life.

Scripture Reading: Matthew 6:9–14

◦◦◦◦ PRAYER FOR TODAY ◦◦◦◦

Father God, I desire to do Your will and live my life in a way that is pleasing to You. Help me to forgive. Help me to release others so that I can be free. Open the eyes of my heart so that I can see myself the way you see me and love others the way You love others. I trust You with my past, present, and future, knowing that You have good things in store for me. In Jesus' Name. Amen.

Open the Door for a Miracle

And whenever you stand praying, if you have anything against anyone, forgive him and let it drop (leave it, let it go), in order that your Father Who is in heaven may also forgive you your [own] failings and shortcomings and let them drop.

Mark 11:25 (AMP)

People have a lot of misconceptions about forgiveness. Some people think they can't forgive because it's just too difficult. The hurt is too deep or the offense is too painful. But in reality, it's more difficult for us when we choose *not* to forgive. Our bitterness is not hurting the person who offended us; it is only embedding itself into our own hearts and keeping us from God's best. Bitterness and unforgiveness block the flow of God's blessing in your life and actually hinder your prayers. But choosing forgiveness opens the door of your heart and makes way for a miracle in your life.

Many people know that in 1981 my mother-in-law, Dodie Osteen, was diagnosed with terminal cancer of the liver and was told she had only a few weeks to live. No medical treatments for the disease were available at that time, and the doctors told her there was nothing they could do. She and her husband, John, went home after they heard the report, got on their knees, and asked God for a miracle. Dodie did everything she knew of in order to be in the position to receive her miracle. Whenever she shares her story, she talks about how one of the main keys to receiving God's healing was her willingness to let go of offenses and keep her heart clean through the power of forgiveness. She tells how she wrote letters of forgiveness to people—her husband, children, parents, or anyone she could think of whom she might have offended or whom might have offended her. She went the extra mile to make sure her heart was free of any offenses that would have blocked God's healing in her life. It took about a year of standing and fighting through all the symptoms, but she did receive her miracle healing and is still 100 percent cancer free today.

It's important to recognize that forgiveness is more than mere words—it's a heart attitude that induces a spiritual transformation. Sometimes we don't necessarily *feel* like forgiving, but when we humbly obey God in this area, He will work a miracle in our lives.

Forgiveness doesn't mean that what the other person did was right or excusable. It doesn't mean that the incident didn't matter. It simply means that you are trusting God to make up the difference and allowing Him to move you past your hurts and pain into your divine destiny. I've heard it said that forgiveness is setting the prisoner free and then realizing the prisoner was you. You can choose freedom today by choosing forgiveness.

Let me encourage you, if someone has wronged you and you still get that cringing feeling on the inside when you see or think about that person, take it to God and allow Him to keep your heart soft and sensitive. Don't let offense keep you from His best. Instead, choose forgiveness and open the door for a miracle in your life today!

Scripture Reading: Matthew 18:21–35

PRAYER FOR TODAY

Father God, thank You for equipping me to overcome in this life. Thank You for the power of forgiveness which sets me free and opens the door for a miracle in my life. I choose Your ways today, I choose peace, I choose love, and I choose forgiveness. Help me to keep my heart and mind open to you and ready to receive every spiritual blessing You have for me. In Jesus' Name. Amen.

God Is at Work in You

[Not in your own strength] for it is God Who is all the
while effectually at work in you [energizing and creating
in you the power and desire], both to will and to work
for His good pleasure and satisfaction and delight.
Philippians 2:13 (AMP)

When we commit our lives to Christ, something supernatural happens on the inside. The God who created the universe chooses to makes His home inside of us and gives us the strength and power we need to accomplish our destiny. The scripture says that God is an "ever-present help." That means no matter what you may be facing today or tomorrow, God is with you, working in you, energizing you, and empowering you to overcome every difficulty so you can live the abundant life He has prepared for you.

The Bible doesn't say that believers will never have any challenges, obstacles, or difficulty; in fact it tells us just the opposite. I've heard it said that the Christian life isn't about the absence of problems; it's about the presence of power—God's power at work in us! In this world we will have trials, but He has already overcome the world and depraved it of power to harm you! When you choose God's ways, you can live in total victory.

Realize that even though life is not always fair, God is always fair. He is a God of justice. It may not be your fault that you are dealing with something; you may have had unfair things happen in your life or a difficult upbringing. God sees every person who has hurt you and every unfair situation that has happened to you. But remember, it's not what happens *to* you but what happens *in* you that matters most. You can choose to allow bitterness, resentment, and unforgiveness to work in you, or you can choose to allow God's power to work in you through forgiveness. Forgiveness starts with a choice. You may not *feel* like forgiving. You may have a lot of questions, hurt, or anger, but when you make the choice to handle things God's way, you'll get God's results—peace, joy, power, freedom, and life.

If we are going to change any part of our lives, we have to start on the inside. Change always begins in the heart when we invite God to work in us. We make the choice; God makes the change. It's okay to say, "God, I don't feel like I can forgive this person, but I'm asking You to give me the grace and the strength to forgive. I am giving my heart to You, and I am giving that person and the situation over to You because You are the only One who can help me forgive and heal my hurts."

If you have been mistreated or disrespected or have experienced a setback in a relationship, on your job, in your finances, or in some other area, don't let that become the major focal point of your life. Instead, choose to look for what God is doing in and through you. What you seek, you will find, and when you look for Him, He'll show up in ways you never dreamed. Be encouraged today because He Who promised is faithful! The good work He began in your life, He will complete. It's not up to you to bring yourself through your difficulty; it's up to you to trust God and let Him bring you through that difficulty. Keep standing, keep believing, and keep praising Him because He is at work in you, energizing you and equipping you to live in victory in every area of your life!

Scripture Reading: Philippians 2:12–18

PRAYER FOR TODAY

Heavenly Father, today I release every care and concern in my life to You. I give you complete control. Even though I may be facing a difficulty, even though unfair things happen, I know You are working in my life. I trust that You are going to bring me to a better place as I keep my heart and mind focused on You. In Jesus' Name. Amen.

Chapter Eight

Enjoying
Rich Relationships

Expectations in Relationships

Love . . . bears all things, believes all things,
hopes all things, endures all things. Love never fails.
1 Corinthians 13:48a (NKJV)

A couple of years ago, I was chatting with a young man who was sharing how the ministry really helped him recover from a terrible divorce. He was saying that he just didn't understand what had gone wrong in his five-year marriage. "After all," he said, "we met through a very reputable matchmaking website. I guess I am living proof that those sites don't really work." He went on to tell how he had filled out the profile and that his computer-matched wife had every quality he desired in a woman. As I listened, I could just imagine him filling out the application much like one might custom-order a car. He wanted a blond woman who loved the outdoors and quiet walks on the beach. Perhaps he also ordered a woman who liked to keep a clean house, cook, and wanted exactly three children—two boys and a girl! He even told me that he was able to request that she be of a certain Christian denomination. Apparently, their problems began during the second year of their marriage when he realized that she didn't really meet all of his standards. He still wasn't sure if she had lied on the profile or changed after they had gotten married, or if the system itself was flawed. He actually said to me, "They never asked 'Are you willing to be there when your husband needs you?' "

This young man is a prime example of how people enter relationships with set standards and expectations. When people don't meet the standards we set, we become disenchanted with the relationship, allowing disappointment and frustration to set in. It's easy to get along with people when everything is going great and others are acting exactly the way we want them to. But what happens when something goes wrong and your feelings get hurt? If you're not careful, you'll begin to focus on the unmet expectations, which will affect your attitude, and ultimately your relationship.

But it doesn't have to be that way if we will just learn to have realistic expectations and let people off the hook. We can avoid a lot of heartache by simply giving people room to be human. We have to accept the fact that nobody is perfect, and even the best people will fail us at times. We have to choose forgiveness because it is not up to anyone else to keep us happy; that is our own responsibility. Too often we want our mate to cheer us up when we are down; we expect our partner to always be loving and kind. We expect our boss to recognize our hard work, and our friends to always be there for us. But those are unrealistic expectations. The perfect spouse does not exist, nor does the perfect boss, nor the perfect friend. We would avoid a lot of disappointments by simply understanding that no matter how much we love people, no matter how much they love us, at some point, they won't live up to our expectations, or they will hurt our feelings in some way. But when we get our eyes off their shortcomings and on to Jesus, we open the door for His grace and healing in our relationships. We open the door for love, which is all that matters in eternity.

Instead of depending on everyone else to make you happy, choose to have realistic expectations and turn your focus to God. Depend on Him to be your source of fulfillment. Remember, God alone can heal your hurts and meet your needs, so put your trust in Him and let Him satisfy you so you can enjoy the people in your life the way God intends.

Scripture Reading: Psalm 118:1–9

⌒⧜⌒   PRAYER FOR TODAY   ⌒⧜⌒

Dear God, today I lift up my eyes to You. You are the One Who can heal and restore me. You are the faithful God who will never leave me and never forsake me. I choose to put my trust and hope in You and ask for your grace to cover me as I extend grace to others. In Jesus' Name. Amen.

Clean the Slate Often

*Love is patient, love is kind. It does not envy,
it does not boast, it is not proud. It does not
dishonor others, it is not self-seeking, it is not
easily angered, it keeps no record of wrongs.*

1 Corinthians 13:4–5 (NIV)

First John tells us that God is love. It doesn't say that God *feels* love, or *has* love; it says that He *is* love. This tells me that love isn't something that just happens when two people are attracted to each other. It isn't something you feel when someone does something nice for you or acts the way you want. And—as I heard someone say one time—love *isn't* something you say to someone just to get something that you want! Contrary to popular opinion, love isn't a feeling at all; love is a state of being. It is a choice. Love will affect our feelings, but ultimately, true love is about choosing God's way of doing things.

First Corinthians, Chapter 13, gives us a picture of what love looks like. It tells us that we choose love by choosing to be patient. We choose love by choosing to be kind. We choose love by being respectful. And among other things, we choose love by letting people off the hook and by keeping no record of the wrongs done to us. Choosing love means "cleaning the slate" in our relationships as often as we can, because holding on to an offense affects the way we see others and drives a destructive wedge in our relationships.

When our son, Jonathan, was a little boy, we bought him a hamster that he affectionately named Hammy. He was so excited. Jonathan loved his furry friend and enjoyed showing him off to his cousins and classmates. Occasionally, he would even let his younger sister hold little Hammy.

One day Jonathan reached into Hammy's cage just as he always did, but evidently that little hamster didn't want to be bothered because instead of jumping into Jonathan's hand as usual, Hammy bit him! Jonathan was shocked. He immediately recoiled his hand— and his heart. From that moment on, he chose to keep his distance from Hammy. You could see the disappointment on Jonathan's face every time he looked at Hammy, but all he could think about was that bite. He would tell his little sister, "Watch out; that hamster might bite you, too! I wouldn't touch him if I were you." Jonathan focused on that hamster bite so much that before long, he forgot all about the fun he used to have with Hammy. He no longer loved that hamster; in fact, he didn't like him at all and we ended up giving Hammy to his cousins.

How many times have we seen this same situation play out in our own relationships? Someone comes into your life, and you really love that person. You have so much fun with your new friend, but then he does something that disappoints you. Your friend doesn't meet your expectations, and you begin dwelling on the negative aspects of the relationship. Before long you've identified every flaw in your friend and decided that that person isn't worth your investment of time and energy. Or you have someone in your life who you've loved for a long time, but one day that person hurts you, much like Jonathan's hamster hurt him, and you simply can't get over it. Every time you look at that person, you relive that hurt all over again. If we are not careful, we will start compiling a mental record of all the times someone has hurt us, and every time that person makes a mistake or disappoints us, we add it to the list. Maybe the same problem comes up repeatedly, and the next time it happens, you have an automatic recording in your mind, *Here we go again.* The next thing you know, you are verbally reciting the list of wrongs or silently rehearsing the offenses in your mind until you are completely frustrated and unhappy.

If you are going to be all that God has created you to be, you have to choose love and be willing to delete the list from your mental files. Just as God promises to forgive and release us, He wants us to forgive and release one another. You have to clean the slate often and make the decision that no matter what someone does, you are not going to hold on to the offense and allow it to pollute your life.

Of course this doesn't mean that you should be a doormat and let people walk all over you. Forgiveness doesn't mean going back into an unhealthy or unsafe situation. Forgiveness doesn't mean automatically putting your trust in people; forgiveness means putting your trust in God to heal and restore you and then follow His peace regarding the direction for the relationship.

Today, are you keeping a record of wrongs done to you? Don't waste another moment of this precious life bound by hurt and offense. Instead, receive His forgiveness and extend it to others so that you can move forward in freedom and victory. Let God's love and forgiveness work in you and wash the slate clean so you can experience the true riches of the relationships in your life.

Scripture Reading: 1 John 4:15–21

⌘⌘⌘ PRAYER FOR TODAY ⌘⌘⌘

Heavenly Father, today I choose Your ways. I choose love because love is all that lasts into eternity. Right now, I release every hurt, offense, and disappointment to You. I ask You to heal my heart and restore my soul. I choose to clean the slate and let go of the past so that I can experience true love, peace, and freedom all the days of my life. In Jesus' Name. Amen.

Making Right Lists

I will consider all your works and
meditate on all your mighty deeds.
Psalm 77:12 (NIV)

At every Lakewood Church service, we have a dedicated time when members and visitors can pray one-on-one with one of our five hundred volunteers who serve as prayer partners. Both Joel and I are prayer partners, and we'll pray for two or three people during the prayer time in each service.

One particular Saturday night, a woman who was about fifty years old came up to me and asked that I pray for her marriage. She told me that her husband had always been hard to live with, and even more so lately. She recited two or three of her grievances, then to my surprise handed me three sheets of notebook paper. She said, "Read this. It is a list of the things he has done, just in the last two weeks."

I opened the pages to see one offense after another scribbled in various colors of ink and pencil. "He's done all this in just two weeks?" I asked.

"Yes," she said. "I didn't think anyone would believe me so I have been writing them down."

"Why so many colors of ink?" I asked.

"Well," she said, "I write them down as quickly as I can so I won't forget them, and I grab the first pen or pencil I can find. If I wait too long, I'll forget." After I prayed for her, I thought, *Wouldn't her life be so much better if she did forget?*

Anytime someone disappoints you or fails to meet your expectations, you have the choice of either dwelling on those disappointments or overlooking them. However, if you *really* want to succeed in your relationship, there is a third choice: You can look past the other person's shortcomings *and* immediately find something about them that exceeds your expectations! Most of the time, you will find dozens of good qualities in a person and only a few things that irritate you. When those irritations come up, pull out that mental list of all the good things that person brings to your life and focus on the benefits of a healthy relationship.

Just after this particular church service, I ran into Richard, another prayer partner in our ministry. He asked, "Did I see you pray for a woman today with a list of things her husband has done wrong?" "Yes," I said. "Do you know her?"

"I prayed for her Wednesday night," he responded. "She showed me the same list. It inspired me to keep a list concerning Lisa."

I was surprised to hear Richard say this because I always thought he and his wife, Lisa, had a good relationship. For a moment, I wasn't sure how to respond. "Oh?" I said, searching for the right thing to say. "Surely Lisa doesn't do that much wrong?"

"No, she really doesn't," he said. "But when she does, I am going to begin keeping a list of all of the things I love about her and all the ways she blesses my life, and I am going to write them down as soon as I think of them, and I'm going to use the first pen I can find."

"So you won't forget them?" I asked.

"So I won't forget them," he answered.

I loved Richard's approach—especially because he drew such a good lesson from such a sad situation. How much better could our relationships be by keeping record of the benefits rather than the shortcomings? After all, that's what God does. He doesn't keep record of what we've done wrong, He keeps record of what we're doing right. Extend that same grace to others. Make "right" lists and watch your relationships grow to a whole new level!

Scripture Reading: Psalm 130:1–4

PRAYER FOR TODAY

Father God, thank You for equipping me and empowering me to love others the way You love me. My greatest desire is to live my life pleasing to You. Help me to extend grace and mercy to others, help me to look beyond their shortcomings and focus on the good things. Bring to mind all of the blessings in my relationships so I can keep my heart focused in the right direction. In Jesus' Name. Amen.

Give Life to Your Relationships

Be an example to all believers in what you say, in the
way you live, in your love, your faith, and your purity.
1 *Timothy 4:12 (NLT)*

Part of having realistic expectations in relationships is under-standing what you can and cannot expect from other people. It's funny because for the most part, people can understand and apply this concept in other areas of everyday life. But when it comes to relationships, our expectations of others seem to rise higher. For example, no matter how badly you may be craving steak and lobster, you know you can't expect to get it from the McDonald's drive-thru because they just don't have it. In the same way, there are some things you can't expect to get from people emotionally because they simply don't have it to give.

If someone never received the affirmation and support they needed growing up, they may not know how to give affirmation and support to others. If your spouse was never encouraged, he may not know how to encourage you today. If your husband doesn't talk a lot or show affection the way you want him to, understand that he may not know how. *You can't expect people to give you what they don't have.* Sure, people can change over time, but they may never be as good at expressing love as you would like them to be.

If you're looking for something different in your relationships, you might begin by looking at yourself. Most times, when you see something missing, you are the one who has it and can bring it to the relationship. *You* carry the seeds of change. If you want more encouragement in your home, sow seeds of encouragement. If you want more affection and tenderness, show affection to others. *Relationships are just as much about what you have to give as about what you are hoping to receive.*

When it comes to showing affection, no two people were more different than my mother and father—at least in the beginning of their relationship. My father grew up in a home where his family did not openly demonstrate their affection. They loved each other very much, but they just expected each other to know it. Their philosophy was that you can love someone, but you don't have to constantly say it. When we would visit, there were hugs when we arrived and when we departed, but there were very few in between. They were wonderful and loving people, but it was just not natural for them to openly display their affection.

My mother grew up quite differently from my father. Her very affectionate Southern family would hug you before you left for the grocery store—after all, you weren't going to see them for at least thirty minutes! When I think back on all of those Christmas holidays and summer vacations we spent with my mother's family, it is the atmosphere of warmth and affection that I remember most. Because of her affectionate upbringing, my mother was the one who brought that atmosphere of warmth into our home. She was always expressive with her love—constantly kissing and tenderly hugging my brother and me. Not a single day went by without her saying that she loved us. We always knew how much we meant to her because she told us so, all the time.

I realize now that my mother's persistent displays of affection profoundly changed my father. Quite simply, she showed him so much affection that he eventually lowered his guard and began to return the affection—not only with her but with my brother and me as well. I'm sure it didn't happen overnight, but once it did, my father was forever changed. I am sure that because of his upbringing, displays of affection did not come as naturally to my father as they did to my mother; however, I would never have known that growing up with him. He never hesitated to show that he loved me, and even today he is warm and affectionate toward me, Joel, and his grandchildren. In fact, he still kisses my brother, Don, on the cheek!

Remember, You have so much to contribute to your relationships. Give your spouse and the people in your life something to draw from. *You* be the model of change. Don't push people to change; instead, lead by example. Dig deep within yourself and plant seeds of love and life into your relationships today!

Scripture Reading: 1 Peter 4:7–11

 PRAYER FOR TODAY

Heavenly Father, today, instead of looking for what I can receive from my relationships, I choose to focus on what I can give. Show me creative ways to invest in others and deposit seeds of life into others. Help me to treasure the people in my life the way You treasure me so I can be an example of your love and life everywhere I go. In Jesus' Name. Amen.

Give People Room to Grow

*Above all, love each other deeply, because
love covers over a multitude of sins.*
1 Peter 4:8 (NIV)

W hen you see someone doing something differently from the way you would do it, do you try to "help" them by offering your advice? What about with your close family? Do you correct them when you know of a better way, or try to straighten them out when you disagree with their methods? Oftentimes, we don't even realize we are doing this, but because we genuinely care about the people in our lives, we want to offer them the wisdom that we've learned over the years. Unfortunately, more often than not, that unsolicited advice actually drives a wedge in the relationship. I see this all the time between husbands and wives, parents and children, and even close friends. Most people already know the areas they need to work on. They don't need you to point out their shortcomings. When we start "fixing" everyone around us, we miss the true riches we were meant to gain from those relationships. When you set out to "fix" someone, what you're really saying is, "You're not good enough the way you are, so I am going to fix you!" But that's not what people need. People need to know they are loved unconditionally. They need to know we approve of them—even when they miss the mark on occasion. They want to know they can count on our love and support no matter what happens. If you find that you are correcting or teaching someone in every conversation, you probably need to adjust your approach with people.

I have to admit, I fell into this habit with my own children. It was not that I was unhappy with them or thought there was anything wrong, I just recognize that there is so little time to impart wisdom into their lives before they are grown and living on their own; I want to pour into them as much as possible. But at one point, I found myself using every moment as a teaching opportunity. One day, I realized that my approach was out of balance. Yes, it's important to instill wisdom and impart good values to our children, but sometimes we have to give them room to grow and learn on their own. It's just as important to listen to them, learn from them, and enjoy them as the people God made them to be. So now I still teach them and impart wisdom, but I balance my instruction with grace and give them the opportunity to grow and learn about life on their own.

The truth is, we've all been guilty of trying to fix, teach, or correct someone else. My own mother used to tell me, "If I could open up your head and pour my knowledge into it, I would." But she couldn't, and neither can I for anyone else . . . and neither can you! Today I encourage you to evaluate how you approach your relationships. Begin by acknowledging the good in the people in your life. Tell them how proud you are of them and how they bring joy to your heart. Use your words to strengthen others and deposit life into them. Give people room to grow because empowering others is what love is all about.

Give People Room to Grow

PRAYER FOR TODAY

Father God, today I choose to honor, respect, and bless the people in my life. I know that You are at work in them in the same way You are at work in me. Help my words to be sweet, wrapped in Your love and grace. Help me to empower and encourage others always, the way You empower and encourage me. In Jesus' Name. Amen.

Bringing Change into Your Relationships

*In kindness he takes us firmly by the hand
and leads us into a radical life-change.*
Romans 2:4 (MSG)

We have a good friend who is a worldwide minister, and years ago when his daughter was in her late teens, she allowed her life to get terribly off course. She started staying out all night and living a very wild lifestyle. Her father was always stern with her, and when she would come home late, he'd be there waiting just to "bust" her and lecture her. This went on month after month, and it didn't seem like anything was getting better. As a matter of fact, it was getting worse.

One day the father was praying and said, "God, when are You ever going to help me with my daughter?" He felt God speak to his heart, "I'm going to help you as soon as you start loving her." The father replied, "God, what do you mean? I do love her with all my heart." God said, "Well then, quit harping on her. Quit threatening to punish her and start showing her that you love her."

From that day forward, this father never said another harsh word to his daughter. He started telling her, "Honey, I love you. I believe in you. I'm proud of you. I know God has something great in store for you." He started speaking words of blessing over her life, and when he changed his approach, she changed her response. It didn't happen overnight, but over several months, this young lady totally turned around her life. She rose to the level of what he spoke over her. He brought change into the relationship by doing things God's way, which set the stage for a miracle.

Do you need to see change in your relationships today? Let it start with you. Ask God to show you how your words and actions can influence the people around you. Whether it's a child, friend, spouse, or coworker, you are a person of influence. Take a moment to think about the way you communicate with others. Are your words uplifting, motivating? Do your actions communicate love and acceptance? Remember, it's God's kindness that leads us to repentance and draws us to change. When you are kind, when you show love to others, you are giving them the grace and strength they need to change and clearing a pathway for them to keep moving forward. When you change the seeds you are sowing into your relationships, you'll change the harvest you are receiving. If you've been sowing seeds of criticism, condemnation, and disapproval, start sowing seeds of life, grace, and encouragement. Just like our minister friend, start loving in new ways. As you do, God's love will shine through you and bring the restoration, hope, and change you've been longing for in your relationships.

Scripture Reading: 2 Corinthians 5:14–21

⌾⟳⟲⌾   PRAYER FOR TODAY   ⌾⟳⟲⌾

Heavenly Father, thank You for Your kindness which leads me to change. Help me to extend that kindness to others. Help me to sow seeds of life, encouragement, and restoration and to empower the people I love. Give me creative ways to show my love for others the way you show Your love for me. Thank You for giving me Your peace, grace, and assurance as I daily follow Your Word. In Jesus' Name. Amen.

Give People the Benefit of the Doubt

Love never gives up . . . Doesn't fly off the handle,
Doesn't keep score of the sins of others, . . .
Puts up with anything, Trusts God always,
Always looks for the best, Never looks
back, But keeps going to the end.
1 Corinthians 13 (MSG)

Life presents plenty of opportunities to become frustrated and upset with people if you allow it. I'm sure you can think of at least one incident this week that opened the door for offense. When this happens, it's easy to place the blame for your frustration and unhappiness on others—"Oh, I'm upset because that person was rude to me." Or, "That person didn't treat me fairly." But the truth is, you are the only person who can determine your own happiness. You have a choice. You can either choose to be offended by people's actions, or you can choose to trust God and overlook offenses.

One way we pick up offenses is by jumping to conclusions. If we would learn to give people the benefit of the doubt and extend grace when we might not see the whole picture, we would have more peace and joy in our day-to-day living. For example, I have a friend who was supposed to meet another friend for lunch one day, but the woman never showed up and my friend wasn't able to reach her by phone. I saw my friend later that day, and I could tell she was upset about it. She thought the woman's actions were very inconsiderate. She told me, "I can't believe her! It's as if she doesn't think my time is as important as hers." The next day, my friend got a call from the woman she was supposed to have lunch with. "I'm so sorry!" she said. "Right as I was about to leave for our lunch appointment, I received a call that my mother was in a terrible car accident and rushed to the emergency room. I was so flustered I forgot to take my cell phone and figured I could call you from the hospital. But by the time I got there, I was so overwhelmed seeing my mother in such critical condition, talking to doctors, and watching monitors—I completely forgot!" My friend immediately forgave her and was so sorry for not giving her the benefit of the doubt.

It all comes down to this: If you want other people to give you grace, then you must choose to extend grace to others. I love what author and speaker Tim Hansel often says: "Give people a break because everybody you meet today is carrying a heavy load." And that's true. We don't know what people are dealing with in their personal lives, but we need each other and we need to encourage and strengthen one another.

Today, don't allow offense to drive a wedge in your relationships. Instead of drawing conclusions, always remember to keep your eyes on Jesus and give the people around you the same grace you receive from Him. Always believe the best of others and choose to give people the benefit of the doubt.

Scripture Reading: Colossians 4:2

⌒⌒⌒ PRAYER FOR TODAY ⌒⌒⌒

Father God, today I lift up my eyes to You because You are my help and strong tower. I choose to receive Your Word and extend Your grace to others. Help me to believe the best and overlook offenses, both real and perceived. Let my words be seasoned with Your love so that I always draw people instead of allowing offense to drive them away. In Jesus' Name, Amen.

Moving Past Disappointments

Then you will know that I am the LORD;
those who hope in me will not be disappointed.
Isaiah 49:23b (NIV)

Everywhere I go, I talk to people who feel "stuck" in life. Maybe they aren't getting anywhere in their job, or they want to move to a new city and can't sell their home, or their relationships aren't what they hoped for. There may be many conditions in the world that can affect our position in life; however, what we see in the natural doesn't set the boundaries for what takes place in the supernatural! God is bigger than every limitation you may face, and He has a plan to take you further than you ever dreamed.

Oftentimes, when people feel like they are stuck, it isn't because of their external conditions; it's because of their internal conditions. Our physical life is often a reflection of what's going on inside of us. If we are stuck in our hurt, bitterness, and negative thinking, it can hold us back in other areas of life, too. That's why scripture encourages us to cast off every weight and every care— because spiritual and emotional weights will hold us back in the natural and keep us from God's best. The good news today is that God has given us the power to move past our disappointments, but the process starts with us, and it starts by our making the choice to focus on the right things.

I once read a story about a woman who was going through a very difficult time in her life. Her mother, with whom she was extremely close, passed away from a sudden heart attack. The woman was devastated and overwhelmed by her mother's death. During her grieving period, many close friends sent beautiful flowers, wrote meaningful cards, and reached out to the family. She knew she needed to write thank-you cards to all the people who had shown such kindness and compassion to her, and eventually she got to the point where she was strong enough to do that.

It took several days, but every morning after getting her son and husband out the door, she sat at the dining-room table and wrote the thank-you notes, pouring out her heart to each person. Writing those notes became a time of healing as she reflected on her life. After four or five days, she finished the notes and gave them to her husband to mail. "If you will mail these for me tomorrow at the office, I can feel free to move forward and start living my life without my mother." He took the letters and said, "Of course I will."

One morning a few weeks later, she saw her husband's tennis bag lying on the floor. Her husband always played tennis after he left the office, and she loved to bless him by preparing his bag with fresh clothes and towels. As she picked up the bag to clean it out, she noticed a big bulge in the side pocket. At first she thought it was some old, sweaty T-shirt stuffed in there, but as she reached into the bag, to her surprise, it wasn't a dirty T-shirt but the bag of thank-you notes she had written several weeks before. Standing there looking at the bag, her heart broke into a million pieces. Feeling betrayed, she thought, *How could this matter so little to him when it matters so much to me?* In her mind, those letters represented her heart, and her husband treated her "heart" like he would his sweaty workout clothes! As she stood there sobbing, her husband walked into the room. With a look of shock on his face, he said, "Oh my . . . I forgot to mail them." He instantly began apologizing and telling her that he would do whatever it took to make it up to her.

He even offered to hand-deliver all the notes himself. He knew he made a major mistake and was so sorry for it. She was devastated, shocked, sad, and angry all at the same time. She felt that she had every right to rant, rave, and make him feel as horrible as she felt at that moment. Nevertheless, somehow, she managed to look him in the eyes, and with an accepting heart, she made the choice to forgive. She thought, *What would it really benefit their relationship to punish him in her time of anger and hurt?*

Instead of holding on to that disappointment and allowing it to keep her stuck in her pain, she chose to focus on the future and the value of her marriage, and she was empowered to forgive and move forward.

We all have a choice in how we deal with our anger and how we respond to the people who have disappointed us. Disappointments are for a season, but our relationships are for a lifetime. Don't get stuck in disappointment; instead, set your focus on what matters most. Keep your eyes on God's eternal plan. Choose forgiveness and choose peace so you can move into the life of blessing and victory He has prepared for you.

Scripture Reading: Isaiah 43:18–26

 PRAYER FOR TODAY

Father God, thank You for giving me the ability to move past every disappointment into life and freedom. I choose to let go of every weight, every care, and every hurt from the past so that I can receive Your peace and healing. Help me to cherish others and overlook their shortcomings. Help me see the good in others so we can move forward in the victory and blessing You have prepared. In Jesus' Name. Amen.

Choose Wise Words

The words of the reckless pierce like swords,
but the tongue of the wise brings healing.
Proverbs 12:18 (NIV)

Joel and I were very young when we married, and like most newly married couples, we had to make some big adjustments. Although we were head-over-heels in love, quite simply, we had to learn to live together. Sometimes irritations would creep in— some small, some large—and before long, those irritations began affecting the way I communicated to my husband. Sometimes I responded in a way that was insensitive or, at the very least, unkind. Several months into our marriage, Joel and I had a disagreement, and instead of letting it go and just agreeing to disagree, I said something that I knew I shouldn't have. I could see those words really hurt him. He no longer wanted to finish the conversation; he simply left the room. As I sat there, I pondered what had just happened. It was then that I felt God speak to me deep down in my spirit. Even as I am writing these words, they are as real to me today as they were that day. He said, "Victoria, if you don't change your words, you're going to change the man you married. Your words are going to cause him to build a wall around his heart, and that will change the foundation of your relationship."

Those words instantly pierced my heart, and tears began to well in my eyes. I was crushed at the thought of negatively affecting my relationship with my husband. I dearly loved him; I loved his gentle spirit, and I didn't want him to change. At that moment, I chose to love and accept Joel exactly the way he was.

I recognized that my hurtful words were the result of allowing myself to focus on the wrong things, little things that didn't even matter. Yet I allowed those little things to compound and upset me so much that it threatened the beautiful relationship we had. Right then, I made the decision to start overlooking those little irritations and to begin focusing on unconditional love and acceptance in our relationship. Instead of getting upset, I took the time to understand my husband and to see his side of things. I chose to magnify the good qualities in him. I chose wise words that brought healing and life into our relationship. As I began overlooking those minor irritations, Joel responded the same way. Even today, the more I treat Joel like a king, the more he treats me like his queen. The more I focus on the good in him, the more he focuses on the good in me. Over the years, we have grown together, we have learned together, and as far as I am concerned, we have built the best relationship in the world.

Today understand that your words, while only puffs of sound, can have a deep and lasting effect on others. Don't let your words cut and wound people's hearts; instead, choose wise words and promote healing. Remember, when we choose our words, we choose either strife or love. It's that simple. Choose love today and invest life, strength, and healing into your relationships.

Scripture Reading: James 3:3–12

⚬~~~⚬ PRAYER FOR TODAY ⚬~~~⚬

Heavenly Father, today I submit my words to You. I choose love by choosing to speak words of life and blessing. Help me to be a vessel of healing, bringing strength and honor to the people around me. Thank You for changing my heart and making me more like You. In Jesus' Name. Amen.

Let Your Love Grow

I pray that your love will overflow more and more,
and that you will keep on growing in
knowledge and understanding.
Philippians 1:9 (NLT)

When I think about my family and the people I love, I feel so blessed. My husband, children, mom, dad, brother, in-laws—I think they're all amazing. But as much as I love them today, I want that love to grow and increase tomorrow. I don't want my relationships to ever become stagnant. I want my love to continue to deepen, so I have to look for new and creative ways to express my love. I have to work toward having stronger, richer connections so that my love influences others for good and always builds them up.

Novelist Katherine Anne Porter once wrote, "Love must be learned, and learned again; there is no end to it." Love should not remain the same year after year; love is supposed to grow. Relationships evolve over time, people change over time, and our love should strengthen and grow over time, too.

The Apostle Paul prayed that our love would abound and grow in knowledge and depth of insight. That tells me that I cannot put my love on autopilot. If we put our love on autopilot and trust that the people in our lives will simply "know" that we love them, our relationships will not grow or be as fruitful as they were intended to be. That's why it's so important to make every effort to stay connected in our relationships and to have purpose in our hearts to let our love grow stronger each and every day.

Several years ago when Joel and I assumed leadership at the ministry, our lives drastically changed and suddenly became more complicated. Oftentimes, we'd find ourselves moving in different directions, so we would both make the conscious effort to keep connected throughout the day. We didn't want to allow our busy schedules to get in the way of growing our love, so we chose to acknowledge each other—to make a connection—each time we passed by each other. Sometimes we'd high-five; sometimes we'd give a quick "I love you" or a kiss. It's not important *how* we connect, but that we *do* connect. We both have a lot going on, but whenever we see each other, everything else is placed on hold for a moment to make that investment in our relationship.

Today I believe God wants to bring you up to new levels in your love and use you to influence the people around you. Even though we can get discouraged at times when others don't respond to our love, we have to choose to trust God and keep loving anyway. Love is such a powerful force, and you can trust that it's working even when you don't see it.

I encourage you to do whatever you can to keep strong connections with the people in your life. Don't let your love switch to autopilot; instead take time to invest in others. Ask God to give you creative ways to show your love, and trust that He is working in your relationships. Make the people you love a priority, keep the connections strong, and build a love that will grow and last into eternity.

Scripture Reading: Philippians 1:3–11

PRAYER FOR TODAY

Heavenly Father, thank You for Your love. Thank You for equipping me to freely love others. Help me to keep the connections strong in my relationships so that my love won't ever become stagnant or cold. Thank You for what You are doing in me and through me. Use me for Your glory today and every day. In Jesus' Name. Amen.

Don't Give Away Your Power

And "don't sin by letting anger control you."
Don't let the sun go down while you are still angry.
Ephesians 4:26 (NLT)

Have you ever thought about how much energy it takes to be bitter or to hold a grudge? We have only a certain amount of energy for each day, and if we use it for the wrong purpose, if we focus on the negative or dwell on whoever hurt us, then we're not going to have the energy we need for the right purposes. We're not going to be able to make the best decisions or be as creative as we need to be. We're not only doing ourselves a disservice, but we're doing our family and our friends a disservice, too.

As much as you may want to, you can't control what other people say or do; you can only control yourself. If you focus on the actions of others and allow them to constantly upset you, then you are handing your peace over to them and giving away your power. The scripture says, "Don't let the sun go down while you are angry." The reason many people don't have joy or enthusiasm is because they go to bed every night with anger and unforgiveness weighing them down. When you go to bed angry, with a cluttered mind, and focused on the negative, you wake up with the same negative emotions . . . not to mention that you probably won't sleep very well, anyway. I heard a story about a couple who had a big fight and were still not talking to each other when they went to bed that night. Since the man didn't want to give in first, he left his wife a note saying, "Wake me up at six o'clock in the morning." The next morning, the man woke up at eight o'clock and was furious because he was so late. He was about to go find his wife and give her a piece of his mind when he noticed a note on his side of the bed that read, "It's six o'clock; wake up."

At one time or another, we have all faced the temptation to disconnect by giving someone the silent treatment or to just go to bed angry. After being married to Joel for more than twenty-two years, I have learned neither of these approaches is the best way to handle a disagreement. You may not reach a resolution by the time the evening comes, but if you will learn how to agree to disagree and still be friends, you will enjoy your relationships a whole lot more and have peace in your home.

I have a friend who told me that sometimes when she and her husband are still mad at each other at bedtime, right before she goes to sleep, she will simply say to him, "I am right, you are wrong, and I love you. Good night."

Of course she is being a little cheeky, but the point is, we should never allow anger and unforgiveness to steal our power and block God's blessing in our lives. We may not always agree with our spouse, family, or loved ones, but we can still choose peace by changing our focus and setting our minds on the good things God has for us.

Remember, if you want to love your life and live it to the fullest, don't let the sun go down on your anger. If you don't have a solution to the issue, agree to disagree and focus on the importance of the relationship. Keep peace in your home, keep joy in your home, keep the connections strong, and don't give away your power!

Scripture Reading: Ephesians 4:20-32

PRAYER FOR TODAY

Heavenly Father, today I release anger, frustration, disappointment, and every negative thing that has happened to me. I choose forgiveness so that I can walk in freedom. I commit to not let the sun go down on my anger, and I choose peace so that I can live in your strength, victory, and power all the days of my life. In Jesus' Name. Amen.

Chapter Nine

Discovering
What Others Need

Study Others

Now also we beseech you, brethren, get to know those
who labor among you [recognize them for what they are,
acknowledge and appreciate and respect them all].
1 Thessalonians 5:12 (AMP)

Having successful relationships begins by knowing well the
people you allow into your life. Too often, people "fill in the
blanks" about others, without really taking the time to see and evaluate their true character. You can't base lifelong commitments on
warm, fuzzy feelings. Instead, take time to study people and understand their strengths as well as their shortcomings, and then decide
if you want to commit yourself to that relationship. You can't go
into a relationship expecting to change the other person; you can
only go into the relationship expecting to change yourself. That's
why it's so important to make sure the other person is someone
you want to adapt yourself to.

Joel and I have been studying each other for a long time. In fact,
I can remember studying him as early as our second date when he
came over to my house for dinner. We were talking in the kitchen
as I was putting the finishing touches on the salad. I started asking
him question after question about various scriptures in the Bible
because, after all, he is John Osteen's son, and I thought he'd want

to talk about spiritual things. Surprisingly, he didn't seem too interested. At one point in the conversation, I asked him about a specific scripture and said, "You probably know where that is found," and handed him a Bible. Joel began flipping through the pages, but before long, he put down the Bible without even answering my "Bible trivia" question. I was stunned! I said, "I can't believe you don't know where that is found! I thought you'd be a spiritual giant." Joel said nothing and just grinned at me as we carried on with the evening.

It wasn't that he didn't know the scripture; he's read his Bible every day since he was a little boy and knows more than I could ever imagine! But Joel was not out to impress me with fancy words and lofty knowledge. He wanted to know my heart and he wanted me to know his. As we continued dating, I took every opportunity to study how Joel treated his family and how he talked about his friends and the people in his life. I observed how disciplined he was and how he was always on time everywhere he went. I noticed how he would always lend a generous hand to the people around him. I took note of the people with whom he surrounded himself and the things he enjoyed doing. I paid special attention to how he treated me and talked to me, and he was always respectful and consistent in his actions. His example meant more to me than if he had quoted the whole Bible!

Actions speak louder than words. If you are single today, take time to watch a person's life before you give them your heart. If you are considering a business deal, take time to learn the person's character before you make a commitment. Don't ignore the red flags. When questionable character issues show up repeatedly, pay attention. Ask yourself, *Could this be telling me something I need to know in the future?* Don't go into a relationship thinking, *Oh that will change down the road.* Chances are, it will change—that character issue will magnify! I remember my father always saying to me, "Victoria, if you don't like something about the person you are going to marry, don't think you can change him when you get married; it will probably only get worse."

Today I encourage you to always be cautious when making commitments in relationships. Study and know well the people you let into your inner circle. You can't go into relationships expecting to change people; you can only go into relationships expecting to change yourself. Be willing to take the time to study others so you can know how to adapt to them and enjoy rich, satisfying relationships the way God intends.

Scripture Reading: 1 Thessalonians 5:12–18

 PRAYER FOR TODAY

Heavenly Father, thank You for giving me a spirit of wisdom and discernment regarding the relationships in my life. Help me to see clearly the people I should allow into my inner circle. Show me how to adapt to the people I love so we can live in blessing and unity and reach our full potential. In Jesus' Name. Amen.

Consider What Others Need

Submit to one another out of reverence for Christ.
Ephesians 5:21 (NIV)

I always chuckle to myself, because I can set my watch by Joel's routine. I know what day he studies to prepare to write his message, and I know what day he writes it. I know when he is going to break for lunch and how long he is going to take to eat it. I know when he is going to come out of his office and what he is going to do after that. He is highly disciplined and precise.

Joel and I mostly work from home. In the mornings, I am busy getting our children ready for school and handling details of the day, so I don't really see Joel much until midday, but whenever I can, I go downstairs and eat lunch with him. When Joel first started preaching and was settling in to his new routine, I naturally assumed that lunchtime would be the perfect opportunity for us to sit down together and catch up on the daily happenings. This worked well Monday through Wednesday, but Thursday was a little different. I noticed that when I would join him on Thursdays, he was not very talkative. In fact, he seemed a bit distant. He would just quickly finish his lunch and go right back to his office. He never said anything to me about it, but I could tell by his actions that he really wasn't looking for conversation.

If I had not already been in the habit of studying Joel and trying to learn about what's important to him, I could have easily become offended or hurt by this scenario, but because I know him so well, I know that Thursday is the day he writes his message for the weekend services. He doesn't want to talk much because his mind is on his message and he doesn't want to lose his focus. There was no need for me to get offended. There was no point in getting upset or trying to change the situation. It wasn't about what *I needed;* it was about what *he needed.* So I stopped coming down to eat with him on Thursdays and didn't make a big deal about it. Joel noticed, though, and he told me later how much he appreciated the way I showed respect for him and his time. It wasn't that big of a deal for me to give up those lunchtime talks one day a week, and it showed Joel that I honored him and that I was willing to adapt to what he needed.

I encourage you today to study the people in your life: your friends, your boss, your spouse, your children. Notice their likes and dislikes. Notice what frustrates them, and observe what makes them happy. Find out what they need and adapt to meet those needs. For example, some people need encouragement when they get stressed out, while others need space and time to process alone. Some people need compliments and affirmation, while others simply need a little quiet time. There's no one-size-fits-all way to relate to people, but if you'll stay open and teachable, God will give you the wisdom to know exactly how to respond. Then, as you adapt to others, you'll find that they will more easily adapt to you, and you'll experience the peace, strength, and unity God designed for your relationships.

Scripture Reading: Ephesians 5:21–33

⌒⌒⌒⌒ PRAYER FOR TODAY ⌒⌒⌒⌒

Heavenly Father, thank You for wisdom to handle my relationships with honor and respect. Help me to adapt and consider what others need. Keep my heart free from offense as I daily choose love and put others first. Thank You for blessing me exceedingly, abundantly, above what I could ever ask or imagine in every area of my life. In Jesus' Name. Amen.

The Importance of White Space

Don't visit your neighbors too often,
or you will wear out your welcome.
Proverbs 25:17 (NLT)

If you've ever taken a design or page layout class you quickly learned the importance of white space. White space is the area on the page where there isn't any text or image. It's the space between the words and the space that makes up the margin. White space helps guide the eye and gives the text some breathing room so you can focus on what's important. Without white space, thewordsonthepagewouldbeverydifficulttoread.

White space is just as important in relationships. We have to give the people in our lives a little breathing room from time to time so they can recharge and be their best. If we are constantly together, constantly talking, constantly in each other's faces, it opens the door for frustration and strife. In order to maximize the "on" time, we have to have some "off" time, too, because it helps us focus on what is really important in our relationships.

For example, when I've had a busy day or I'm feeling overwhelmed, Joel can always sense it, so he'll do something like take the kids out to dinner or to their cousins' house so I can have some time to myself. He knows I like to take a hot bubble bath or get my nails done or simply escape to the mall for a while. It's amazing what an hour of "white space" at the mall will do for a woman, isn't it!? The point is, having time to myself reenergizes me and makes everything else I do more manageable.

Joel is the same way; he needs time to unwind and relax as well, although when he wants to recharge his batteries, he likes to sit in his big chair in the bedroom and watch *Wheel of Fortune.* Quite often, when he wants to get his mind off things, he plays outside with the kids or plays a game of basketball with some of the guys. Either way, I am happy to give him what he needs because I know that it is a small investment with a big return.

To make the most of our relationships, we have to be willing to give the people in our lives what *they* need, which may not necessarily be what *we* need. When I need to be refreshed, Joel doesn't tell me to go play kickball in the backyard with the kids. He doesn't say, "That's what I do, so you should do it, too." In the same way, when he needs to clear his mind, the last thing I would suggest is for him to go to the mall. Joel and I both know how important it is to be considerate of each other's needs, so we make every effort to study and adapt to each another.

Maybe today, when you see your spouse after a long day at work, instead of bombarding him with all of your requests, be patient and give him some time to unwind. The same is true for children. They may not want to answer twenty questions the first minute you see them after school. Instead, wait until they have a snack and settle down, then ask them how their day went. If you will look for the best opportunity and wait for the right time, you will have much more success and much less tension in your relationships.

Today I encourage you to consider what others need and give them the space to recharge. Even Jesus had to take time to be alone, and if Jesus needed "white space," we can be sure that all of us need it, too!

Scripture Reading: Luke 5:12–16

⟬⟭ PRAYER FOR TODAY ⟬⟭

Heavenly Father, thank You for giving me wisdom to handle my relationships carefully. Help me to love others and honor them by Your grace. Teach me to understand the needs of the people I love, and show me how to meet those needs and sow good seeds into my relationships. In Jesus' Name. Amen.

Improving Communication

A word fitly spoken is like apples of
gold in pictures of silver.
Proverbs 25:11 (KJV)

One thing I've learned is that if you want to communicate effectively in your relationships, you have to study others and learn about their communication style. Some people want all the details before they can make a decision, and to others, all those details are overwhelming and distracting; they only want to hear the most important details. If we will study the people in our lives and adapt to their communication style, our words will be received better and we'll be better equipped to grow and move forward together.

One time I was enthusiastically telling Joel something that I thought was important, and just as I was getting to the good part, I noticed his eyes beginning to glaze over. I began talking faster and faster, but it didn't do any good. Finally I said, "You don't want to hear this; I can tell because you are not even paying attention to me." It wasn't anything he said; it was how he looked. He obviously had something on his mind already, and I could tell by his body language that I had lost him after the first three minutes. At first my feelings were a little hurt and I got frustrated, thinking, *I am not telling him anything anymore.* But, of course, I didn't mean it. Instead, I adjusted my communication style with him; now I try to tell him only the most important details of the story. When I see his eyes glazing over, instead of taking it personally and getting upset, I recognize it as my cue that he is going into "detail overload," and I simply adapt my communication style.

I was explaining the principle to a woman and she asked, "Victoria, why would you change yourself in order to please Joel?" The truth is, I'm not changing who I am; I'm changing the way I communicate so I can have a better relationship with my husband. I want Joel to hear me, so I adapt my delivery to the way he listens best. It is good for me and good for him.

Another way to improve communication in your relationships and to help the people around you understand you better is by simply telling them what you need. The people in your life can't read your mind. You can't always expect them to know exactly what you want or need. You should respectfully express what you like and dislike and tell them kindly what helps you and what bothers you. When I want to discuss something with Joel, I tell him in advance, "I don't want you to try to solve my problem. I just want you to hear me out, because that will help me to work it out." All I need is for him to lend a supportive ear. Knowing this, he does his best to listen as I get my thoughts out in the open. Because Joel has an understanding of what I need and I have an understanding of what he needs, it keeps the tension out of our relationship and helps us appreciate each other.

Relationships are all about learning. In marriage we are learning to become one; in families we are learning to get along; in business we are learning to work together; in friendships we are learning to make allowances for one another. Life is a learning process, and the quicker you embrace that fact, the more you'll enjoy the people around you. Start today by becoming a student of your relationships. Choose to make your communication as effective as possible by extending grace and adapting to what others need.

Scripture Reading: Proverbs 25:11–20

⌒⚬⚬⚬⚬⌒ PRAYER FOR TODAY ⌒⚬⚬⚬⚬⌒

Heavenly Father, help my words to be like apples of gold in settings of silver. Help me to communicate in a way that is effective and received by others. Give me wisdom to adapt and to improve the way I relate to the people I love. Thank You for peace, joy, and discernment to make wise choices so that my relationships can be the very best they can be. In Jesus' Name. Amen.

Be Fully Engaged

Let the wise listen and add to their learning . . .
Proverbs 1:5 (NIV)

Years ago we were on a family vacation, just enjoying ourselves and unwinding when I said, "Isn't it great to just relax and not have to run around and do anything?"

Alexandra, our daughter, spoke up and said, "Yeah, vacation is great because when Jonathan and I say something funny, Dad doesn't give us his *courtesy laugh*."

"Courtesy laugh—what does that mean?" I asked.

"You know . . . when he's busy and not really paying attention and we say something funny, he just says, 'Ha!' But, when he is relaxed, he always gives us a real laugh and says something funny back to us."

This simple story is a great reminder to us all that people can tell when we are fully engaged and want to hear what they are saying; and they can also tell when we are preoccupied and distracted. I believe part of being respectful and considerate to others is to listen attentively and to be fully engaged in every conversation. We should always make the effort to give the other person our undivided attention, look them in the eyes, and show a genuine interest.

I've found this to be especially important with children. I recognized early on that my children have a need to be heard, so I have learned to be creative when communicating with them. I give them the opportunity to share their feelings and explain their points of view to me. It's important that they know that I value and respect what they have to say. When we have open dialogue, it builds trust and it's much more productive than simply saying, "The answer is no—just because I said so!"

I'm not saying that you have to justify every parenting decision or have a long, drawn-out conversation every time you say something to your children, but you can always find a way to present your point in a positive, educational way. If you have teenagers in your house, you know how important it is for them to be heard; don't shut them down with, "It's not up for discussion." Sometimes, for teenagers, it isn't about getting their way; they simply want to be heard and know that you value their viewpoint. When you listen to your children and give them your full attention, you are building their confidence and making them feel important and loved.

No matter what the age, everyone has a deep need to be valued and respected. When people are talking to you, don't interrupt them. Let them finish their thoughts. You may already know what they're going to say, but that's okay; be considerate and let them finish anyway. If someone asks you a question, and you know the answer before she finishes speaking, resist the tendency to jump in and cut her off with a, "Here, let me tell you what to do." Listening is not only a matter of being considerate but also of letting the speaker know you really care.

Today, choose to give the gift of listening. Be fully engaged. Scripture says that when you listen to others, you grow in wisdom. Sow those good seeds into your relationships, value the people you love, and open the door for a wonderful harvest of blessing in return.

Scripture Reading: Isaiah 50:4–5

PRAYER FOR TODAY

Heavenly Father, thank You for leading and guiding me and for giving me discernment regarding the relationships in my life. I want to be fully engaged and show respect to others. Help me, by Your Spirit, to be a good listener and to always give my best to the people I love. In Jesus' Name. Amen.

Find Common Ground

Can two walk together, unless they are agreed?
Amos 3:3 (NKJV)

We all encounter difficult people from time to time. You might even have someone coming to mind at the mention of the word "difficult." Chances are that person is in your life for a reason, either to make you better or to give you the opportunity to help him or her become better. Scripture says that iron sharpens iron . . . and when it does, sometimes sparks fly!

One way to overcome negativity in a difficult relationship is by finding common ground. Whether it's a family member, a co-worker, or an unhappy person you encounter at the grocery store, if you make the effort, you can actually get along with most people. It may take a little practice and creativity, but the end result is worth it. Common ground can involve just about anything—maybe you went to the same college or you both enjoy the same hobby. Maybe you both like animals or have a mutual friend, or shop at the same store or like the same foods. It doesn't actually matter what the thing is that you do have in common. The point is, when you find something you both agree on, it creates common ground and turns a potentially stressful interaction in a positive direction.

Sometimes, finding common ground means saying nothing at

all and simply smiling so you can stand on the common ground of peace. This is especially true when you're in a conversation with someone whose views differ from yours. Sometimes, for the sake of peace, you have to let go of your need to be heard. Joel is really good at finding the common ground of peace. I remember one time, Joel and I were talking to an acquaintance we hadn't seen in a while, and the man began telling us some stories and sharing his strong opinions about a particular subject. As Joel and I listened to this man, I thought, *I don't agree at all with what this man is saying.* The man went on and on, and I knew Joel couldn't possibly be agreeing with him either, but Joel just stood there with his trademark smile on his face, nodding and engaging with this man the best way he could. Finally it was time for us to leave, and Joel and I wished him well.

After we walked away, I said, "Joel, I don't know why you didn't give him your opinion. I know you don't agree with him."

Then Joel said something I will never forget: "Victoria, *I wasn't put on this earth to straighten everyone out.*"

That day I received wisdom that will be with me forever—it's not my job to straighten everyone out, it's my job to pursue peace. We need to learn that other people have a right to their opinions. We don't have to say everything we think all the time. We don't have to be right or always prove our point. Of course, there may be times when it's appropriate to share your views and wisdom with someone, but that's very different from constantly sharing your opinions. Most times, you'll get a lot more accomplished and live a happier life by holding your tongue and standing on the common ground of peace.

Today I encourage you to step out and look for common ground with someone who has been difficult to get along with. Remember, when you find common ground, when you are kind and compassionate, you have a much better chance of influencing people's opinions and speaking into their lives. When you are pursuing peace, it's not about who's right; it's about what's right and working together toward a common goal. Remember, no matter how

241

different your backgrounds, no matter how different your views and opinions, you can have peace and harmony in relationships simply by finding common ground.

Scripture Reading: Psalm 34:8–14

PRAYER FOR TODAY

Father God, You said in Your Word that peacemakers are blessed, and today I choose blessing by choosing to be a peacemaker. Help me to always take the high road and look for ways to connect with others by finding common ground. Give me discernment to know when to speak and when to hold my tongue. Let Your love continue to work in me so that I can be an example of You everywhere I go. In Jesus' Name. Amen.

Empowered Through Unity

How good and pleasant it is when God's people
live together in unity! . . . For there the LORD
bestows his blessing, even life forevermore.
Psalm 133:1–3 (NIV)

I heard a story about a young man who was hired as a server at an upscale restaurant. Even though he was starting as an assistant waiter, he was excited about his job and the opportunity to advance to a headwaiter. He soon discovered that the headwaiter to whom he reported was a very difficult woman. She was the top producer and had built a loyal customer base, but there was a reason for her unusual success. It turns out she didn't have much competition— she was so sarcastic and condescending to all the other waiters that they would usually end up quitting before they had a chance to be promoted. She was starting to use those same bullying tactics on this young man. She would intentionally mess up his orders and do whatever she could to try to get him in trouble.

The young man really needed his job, so he decided he would not allow this woman to get the best of him. He knew the easy route would have been to quit and find another job, but he chose to stay and try to win her favor. One day he overheard her talking to one of her customers about her "babies." He thought to himself,

I didn't know she had children. So he decided to wait for the best opportunity to ask her about them. When he did, he found out those "babies" were actually her two cats, and they meant the world to her. The young man had grown up with a cat in his home, and when he mentioned it, her face totally changed; he saw an opening into her heart. Day after day, he would ask about her cats and listen intently as she told him all about their quirky personalities. That young man found common ground with the woman, and before long she and he had a wonderful working relationship. He even stayed at the restaurant long enough to achieve his goal of advancing to headwaiter himself! Because the young man chose to sow seeds of kindness rather than treat the woman the way she was treating him, God opened a door of opportunity, and the young man was able to eventually reap a harvest of blessing in his own life.

Sometimes we have to go that extra mile to find common ground with another person. I've discovered that if you will take the time to identify with the people you encounter throughout the day, everything will go more smoothly, and your life will become more pleasant. When you encounter a difficult person and start to cringe inside, right then, you have a choice to make: you can *react* to that person or *respond* to them. If you react, you're allowing *them* to decide your actions, and you'll probably end up doing or saying something you'll regret later. But when you choose to respond, *you* choose your actions—you can take the high road and overlook the other person's negative attitude.

Remember, when we choose peace, we are honoring God and setting ourselves up to receive His blessing. The next time you run into a difficult person, turn that situation around for good by finding common ground, and be empowered through unity.

Scripture Reading: James 3:13–18

⟨❦⟩ PRAYER FOR TODAY ⟨❦⟩

Heavenly Father, thank You for the blessing of unity. Thank You for empowering me to rise above difficult situations as I choose peace. I know that my struggles in this life are not against flesh and blood, so I lift up my eyes to You because You are my source of strength and help. Have Your way in me as I submit myself to Your Word. In Jesus' Name. Amen.

The Power of Kindness

Be kind to one another . . .
Ephesians 4:32 (NAS)

It's amazing what can happen when you are kind and considerate to others. Whether it's a friend, family member, or even a total stranger, by simply being kind you can open the door for God's favor and kindness to be poured back onto you.

A while back, my brother, Don, was looking for a new car and thought he had found the one he wanted. The salesman needed to get him some additional information, so Don gave the man his phone number to follow up with him. Several days went by and Don didn't hear back from the salesman. In the meantime, after considering some of the car's features, his interest waned, and he eventually changed his mind and decided against purchasing it.

One evening, as Don was just starting to relax after a long day at work over a wonderful bowl of hot noodle soup—his favorite on a cold night—his daughter came running over with the phone. "Daddy, Daddy! There's someone on the phone for you."

Reluctantly, Don took the call, only to discover that it was the salesman from the car dealership. As soon as he said hello, the salesman started going on and on about the car Don had looked at more than a week before. Don was trying to be as nice as possible and said, "Thank you, but I've decided that car is not big enough, and I have changed my mind." The salesman went on and on about how great the car was, as if he didn't even hear what Don had said. Don just sat there staring at that big bowl of noodles—getting cold—trying to be as nice as possible.

"Sir, I've changed my mind about that car," Don said, but the man just continued to try to talk Don into that car.

"Would you like to speak with my sales manager?" he asked.

Don took a deep breath and had several responses rolling around in his head when suddenly he heard himself say, "Yes."

Immediately, he thought, *Did I just say yes?* During the brief moment of silence, he kept reminding himself to be nice and courteous even though all he really wanted to do was hang up so he could enjoy his dinner!

The manager got on the phone, introduced himself, and said, "I just want to ask you a question—"

"Thank you," Don replied, "but really, I've changed my mind about that car."

The manager interrupted, "Are you Victoria Osteen's brother?" he asked.

"Yes," Don responded.

The manager continued, "I go to Lakewood Church, and even if you don't want that particular car, I want to help you find the car you want and get you the very best price possible."

Don hardly knew what to say, but he was grateful he had chosen to be kind and courteous! Because of his response, God was able to bring him a divine connection. Several weeks later, the sales manager found Don the car he really wanted and gave him a price he could hardly believe.

Romans 2:11 says, "God does not show favoritism." He'll show you the same favor if you'll choose to be kind and respectful to people. Regardless of whether you are dealing with your spouse, children, grocery clerk, or a salesman on the phone, remember you are God's representative. Be courteous, gentle, and kind to others and keep the door open for God to pour out His blessings on your behalf.

Scripture Reading: Titus 3:1–11

PRAYER FOR TODAY

Father God, thank You for the power of kindness. I invite You to fill me with Your love today so I can treat others with respect and honor the way You command. Empower me by Your Holy Spirit to always take the high road, always believe the best, and always choose love. Thank You for doing a work in me and through me. In Jesus' Name. Amen.

Chapter Ten

Being a People Builder

Pour Life into Others

Let this same attitude and purpose and [humble]
mind be in you which was in Christ Jesus:
[Let Him be your example in humility:]
Philippians 2:5 (AMP)

Like a mirror, the Bible tells us that we should reflect the character and likeness of Jesus. We should have His same attitude and follow His example. Now that may sound like a pretty tall order; after all, Jesus was the Son of God. But remember, when we accept Him as our Lord and Savior, we become sons and daughters of the Most High God, too. We become empowered by the same Spirit that raised Christ from the dead! That means we have the same spirit of humility—the same strength, the same love, and the same power on the inside. We are equipped to follow His example and do what He did. What did He do? The scripture says that when Jesus walked the earth, He went around doing good and bringing healing to others, physically, spiritually, and emotionally. He poured life into others everywhere he went!

I recently read a children's book that illustrated this concept. The premise of the story is that we each carry an invisible, emotional bucket. When your bucket is full, you feel happy, satisfied, and encouraged; when your bucket is empty, you feel down and discouraged. In this world, there are "bucket fillers" and "bucket dippers." A bucket filler is a person who follows the example of Christ and adds to others by encouraging and investing in them with kind words and actions. When bucket fillers are pouring life into others, they soon find that their own buckets are filled up, too. Bucket dippers, on the other hand, are those who take away from people by using harsh or negative words. They not only deplete other people's buckets, but they also diminish the contents of their own.

God intends for us to be bucket fillers, using our lives and resources to pour life into others and help them be the very best they can be. I think about Peter, one of the disciples of Jesus. He was impulsive; he said things he shouldn't have, and he needed to grow in many areas. Despite Peter's personality drawbacks, Jesus referred to him in surprisingly positive terms. He said, "Peter, you are a rock." Simon Peter's very name meant "pebble," and I wonder if he felt like a tiny pebble at times, especially after some of his foolish blunders. Nevertheless, Jesus reminded Peter of what he was becoming—a solid, stable rock. He spoke potential and confidence into Peter's life. He poured life into him, and we should follow this example in our relationships as well. Let's be bucket fillers, not bucket dippers. Instead of reminding the people in our lives of their failures and faults, let's see the solid rock in them and speak positively about what they are becoming.

What are you doing to pour life into your loved ones? Whether you are a natural encourager or you feel a bit uncomfortable giving compliments, you possess a unique ability to make others feel better about themselves. The truth is, we all have different personalities and different ways of relating to one another, but we can all become great encouragers. I truly believe encouragement is one of the best gifts we can give other people.

Scripture tells us to "Encourage one another daily." That's because throughout the day, we have opportunities to get discouraged. We face difficulties; plans don't always work out; life has a way of stealing our joy. Every one of us needs our emotional buckets to be filled up and refilled on a regular basis. A simple compliment or a kind word really can make someone's day! Not only do positive words lift up others, but I've found that encouraging words are the glue that holds our relationships together. Looking back over the last twenty-two years in my marriage, I can see how positive words and regular affirmations have bonded Joel's and my hearts together and have caused us to bring out the best in each other. We've learned the importance of encouraging each other daily—not just through our words but also through simple acts of kindness and finding ways to make life easier for each other. You can do the same in your relationships and improve the atmosphere of your household, your workplace, your community, and your world.

Sure, it takes effort to be a great encourager, but when you bring out the best in others and help them succeed, that success *will* come back to you and cause you to rise higher as well. When you fill the emotional buckets of others, God will make sure to fill your bucket in return.

Scripture Reading: Romans 12:9–21

 PRAYER FOR TODAY

Heavenly Father, I invite you to dwell in my thoughts, heart, and attitude. I choose to follow Your example and bring good to others. Help me to be a pure reflection of Your love in everything I do, as I look for ways to pour life into others. In Jesus' Name. Amen.

The Weight of Your Words

*The tongue has the power of life and death,
and those who love it will eat its fruit.*

Proverbs 18:21 (NIV)

Scripture tells us that our words contain the power of life and death. You have the power to speak life into your home and into the people around you, and you were given that power for a reason. The people around you need to hear your words of encouragement. Sometimes we compliment strangers or people we barely know more than we compliment our own family members! Many times, a person will tell a coworker what a great job she did, but when her own spouse excels, she doesn't say a word. But we should always compliment and encourage our own family members as much as we do others—if not more.

People often compliment Joel after he speaks, saying something such as, "Joel, that message was really great. You've helped change my life." Those are meaningful words of encouragement for him, but I have learned that they don't have nearly as much impact on Joel as my words of affirmation. As a spouse, as a family member, recognize that your words carry greater weight. Sometimes, I'll look over at Joel on Sunday evening and say, "Joel, you're always good, but that message was especially great today." I know how important it is to recognize his hard work and dedication, so I will often mention a specific point I liked in his message. I can see how that encourages him and lets him know I appreciate his gifts and talents. Even though he may have heard numerous compliments from other people that day, my words take deeper root because God designed it that way.

It's easy to take the people closest to us for granted. "I don't need to say anything to them," you might say. "They know I love them. She knows I think she is beautiful. He knows I think he is great." Maybe so, but a blessing is not a blessing until it is spoken. When you release those positive, faith-filled words of affirmation, they will have a positive effect in the lives of the people you love. I am convinced that when we put family first, when we take the time and make the effort to be good to our family members and give them our best, then all the other relationships in our lives will improve as well.

I heard about a woman who said to her husband one day, "Honey, do you really love me?"

He looked at her strangely and said, "Why would you ask me that? I told you that I loved you the day I married you thirty-five years ago. If it ever changes, I'll let you know."

The truth is, the phrase "I love you" can never be heard enough in our homes. We can't take for granted that the people we love automatically know it. Are there people close to you who need to hear those three little words? Begin to say them today. Maybe you weren't raised in an expressive environment, but why don't you be the one to start a new tradition? You can affect your family line for generations to come. What better legacy to leave than a legacy of love, kindness, and encouragement.

I was discussing the power of encouragement with one of my friends one afternoon, and she said something I thought was right on. She shared, "When I brag on my husband, I can see a change in him. He rises to the occasion and strives to go to new levels. But when I nag at him or say nothing at all, he's more complacent and doesn't have the passion and enthusiasm to accomplish what is in his heart."

That's true for all of us. Nagging only make things worse, but encouraging words will put people on their feet and bring out the best in them. We should always look for opportunities to speak words of blessing over the people around us. When your spouse gets a promotion at work, take time to say, "I knew you could do it! You're amazing!" When your child comes home with good grades, even if they are less than *you* had hoped, don't be too busy to celebrate. Stop and say, "I am so proud of you. Way to go!" When your mother fixes Sunday dinner for the whole family, tell her, "Mom, I know that's a lot of work, but your hospitality means so much." When your coworker loses fifteen pounds, don't be jealous; congratulate her with a compliment.

Remember, the people in your inner circle not only *want* your approval—they *need* it. Life and death is in the power of your tongue, and the seed you sow will produce a harvest for your future. Speak words of faith and victory to your loved ones, and set yourself up for a harvest of victory in your own future.

Scripture Reading: James 3:2–12

 PRAYER FOR TODAY

Father God, I recognize that I carry the power of life and death in the words that I speak. I choose today to speak life-giving words and to sow good seeds for my future. Keep my heart and mind open to seeing the best in others. Give me words of faith, blessing, and encouragement to help people rise up and move forward into the victory You have prepared. In Jesus' Name. Amen.

Showing Honor

Be devoted to one another in love. Honor
one another above yourselves.
Romans 12:10 (NIV)

Showing honor is a major key to enriching our relationships and opening the door for God's honor and blessing in our own life in return. All throughout scripture, you'll find promises and blessings for people of honor. In fact, the first commandment in the Bible that carries a promise is to honor your parents so that you can have a long, happy life.

Honor can be displayed in many ways, but at its most basic level, honor treats someone with respect or gives them special recognition. Showing honor is a choice, and we need to look for opportunities to honor the people in our lives.

Words of affirmation show honor, and they draw people close to you and help them see the best in themselves. For example, if you have a friend who is really good at organization, encourage her to use that talent. You might say, "You are such a great organizer. In fact, you could probably make a business out of your organizational skills. I'd hire you for sure!" That simple expression of encouragement, honor, and recognition could be the seed of affirmation that causes her to believe in herself and go after her dreams. Rather than condemning people for what they are doing wrong, let's strive to catch people doing what is right and compliment and reward them with encouraging words.

Showing honor and respect for someone isn't just about recognizing their accomplishments and abilities. You can honor someone simply by acknowledging and esteeming them for who they are. Years ago when a friend from another state was visiting me, I introduced her to some of my friends and family, including the husband of a well-known woman in the community who is regularly on television and often the center of attention. When I introduced this man to my friend, I purposely didn't introduce him as "so-and-so's" husband. Instead, I introduced him by name and then simply stated that *she* was married to him. I noticed a pleasant look of surprise on his face. He put his shoulders back and seemed to enjoy the fact that someone recognized who he was and took the time to make him feel important. Just that little change of syntax can make all the difference. It showed him respect and let him know that I valued him for who he was as an individual—not just as a well-known person's husband.

Another way to show honor and respect is through small acts of kindness. We all like different things, or to put it another way, we don't all like the same things. Find out what makes the people in your life feel special. Oftentimes, we think we have to plan a major surprise that takes weeks of organizing in order to really make an impact. It's great if you are able to pull off something outlandish, but I've found that small acts of kindness on a regular basis often have just as much, or even more, impact. For example, Joel knows that I love one cup of coffee every morning. Although he doesn't drink coffee, he knows *I* love it and he takes time to make it for me every day—and quite often he even brings it to me in bed! Usually Joel gets up earlier than I do, and when I go into the kitchen and see my coffee already made, that lets me know that Joel was thinking about me. When he got up, I was on his mind. Making the coffee doesn't take him two minutes; it's not hard; it's not expensive; yet it lets me know that he values and honors me. That small act of kindness shows he honors me and it draws us closer together.

What acts of kindness can you show someone today? How can you go out of your way to show respect and love? Remember, little things mean a lot. Find ways to honor others; when you do, you leave a lasting impression on their hearts.

Scripture Reading: Exodus 20:2–12

 PRAYER FOR TODAY

Father God, today I choose to be a person of honor. I want to show love and respect to others in a way that builds them up and is pleasing to You. Open the eyes of my heart and help me to see others the way You see them. In Jesus' Name. Amen.

Writing on the Hearts of Others

My tongue is the pen of a ready writer.
Psalm 45:1 (NKJV)

Genesis tells us that when God created the heavens and the earth, He spoke them into existence. Because we are made in His image, scripture tells us that the same power to create is in our words, too. I like to think of it this way: We are all artists with our words and we paint on the canvas of people's hearts by what we speak, good or bad. That's why we need to be careful to use our words wisely, as a skillful artist would, creating a positive, encouraging masterpiece in the hearts of our family members, friends, and coworkers.

A beautiful work of art isn't created by merely choosing the right paint colors; it's created by the technique of the artist as well. In the same way, we have to be just as careful with *how* we communicate as we are with *what* we communicate.

Years ago, I learned this lesson the hard way when I was trying to encourage our son, Jonathan, to practice his guitar. I was driving the kids home from school one day and thinking about all the loose ends I'd left dangling on that particular afternoon. You might say I was feeling a bit stressed, and I let that stress come right through when I sharply asked, "Jonathan, have you practiced your guitar at all this week?" Before he could answer, I continued, "You know, if you don't practice your guitar now, you'll be sorry down the road when you want to play in the band at church and you're not good enough."

On and on I went, trying to "encourage" my eleven-year-old son to practice his guitar with enthusiasm and passion, and yet I could see his countenance deflating and becoming more discouraged by the minute. All at once, I started listening to my own words, which really weren't encouraging or inspiring at all. In fact, they were rather discouraging. When I realized that I was painting a negative picture on the canvas of his heart, I immediately stopped myself and said, "Jonathan, I'm sorry. I realize I wasn't very encouraging just now. Will you forgive me?"

I looked at him in the rearview mirror, and he just smiled at me so sweetly. Right then, I decided to use my words to paint a picture of inspiration not condemnation. I said, "Jonathan, you are so talented musically. That's why I want you to practice, because I know the more you practice, the better you'll become . . ." I repackaged my words and changed my voice from the voice of discouragement and defeat to the voice of encouragement and victory.

Just like anything else, it takes practice to become a skillful "painter" with your words, but you can do it! Even when you have to bring correction or instruction, you can position your words so they will be more easily received. Just like the old saying goes, "a spoonful of sugar helps the medicine go down," when you speak words of affirmation along with the correction, it's all much more palatable and will have a greater impact.

When you realize the impact of your words, you'll seize every opportunity to paint positive images on your loved ones' hearts. Look for chances to say, "I'm behind you. I'm supporting you. I'm with you every step of the way." Whether you're a boss working with an employee or a parent working with a child, the goal should always be to help others reach a higher level. Proverbs tells us that reckless words pierce like a sword so you must never allow harsh words to cut the canvas you are working on! Instead, "sweeten" your delivery, be the voice of victory, and create a masterpiece on the hearts of the people you love.

Scripture Reading: Hebrews 10:19–25

⟡⟡⟡ PRAYER FOR TODAY ⟡⟡⟡

Father God, what an awesome responsibility You've given me with the power of my words. I choose to use my words to bring life and paint a beautiful masterpiece on the hearts of the people I love. Help me to hear Your voice and speak Your truth so I can be a blessing everywhere I go. In Jesus' Name. Amen.

The Gift of Listening

Understand this, my dear brothers and sisters:
You must all be quick to listen, slow to speak,
and slow to get angry.

James 1:19 (NLT)

A few years ago, I was at the church and deeply engaged in conversation with a woman while my little girl, Alexandra, was standing beside me and really wanting my attention. This woman was pouring her heart out to me, and I didn't want to cut her off midsentence, but Alexandra was tugging on my pant leg, desperate for my attention.

I started to get frustrated with my daughter, but instead of acting on that feeling, I decided to make a positive deposit into her heart. I interrupted the woman very respectfully and said, "Just one minute. I need to speak with my daughter, but I really want to hear the rest of your story." Then I knelt down beside Alexandra and looked attentively into her big blue eyes and whispered, "I know you want to talk to me right now, but I am already speaking with this woman, and I can't listen to both of you at the same time. Honey, what you have to say is so important to me, I don't want to miss one single word of it, so give me two minutes to finish up, and I'll give you my full attention."

Alexandra smiled at me and nodded in agreement. In fact, her whole countenance changed because she felt so important. She stood a little taller and prouder knowing that I truly wanted to listen to her. That deposit in her life let her know how much she mattered to me. She knew that she would have her mother's undivided attention in a few minutes, and she was content to wait.

It's easy to get busy in life, and if you're like me, you can listen and work at the same time. We call it multitasking, but sometimes multitasking isn't the best use of our time. Sometimes we have to stop, look someone in the eyes, and give the gift of listening. We need to take time to deposit value in their hearts. We need to support one another, and listening is an amazing way of doing just that.

As you go about your day, remember to give people the gift of listening. It seems like such a little thing, but those little deposits will eventually make a big difference. When you make deposits in people, you are making deposits in eternity, and that is what pleases the heart of God. Maybe no one took the time to invest in you this way when you were growing up, but if you listen carefully, God is constantly speaking words of affirmation into your heart. He created you to be a winner, and He wants to help you learn to communicate that message to the people around you. It's never too late to change how you communicate. Start by taking time to listen to God with your heart and He will equip you to listen and pour into others.

Scripture Reading: James 1:19–25

⌘⌒⌒⌒⌒⌒ PRAYER FOR TODAY ⌒⌒⌒⌒⌒⌘

Father God, thank You for loving me and for listening to me when I call upon Your Name. I desire to pour life into others and be a blessing to the people I love. Help me to be slow to speak and quick to listen so that I can invest in others the way You have invested in me. In Jesus' Name. Amen.

Creating a Winning Atmosphere

*Keep each other's spirits up so that no
one falls behind or drops out.*
Ephesians 6:13 (MSG)

A while back, I was having a conversation with a woman and her husband. She was jokingly telling me, "In my house, I am always right."

Her husband chimed in, "She lives to be right! She challenges everything we say," referring to himself and their children.

"He just hates that I'm always right," she said with a big smile on her face.

Now, this *could* have been funny . . . except that she wasn't kidding. She didn't recognize that her desire to be right all the time was driving home the point that everyone around her was wrong. She was creating a losing environment for her husband and children and depleting their sense of worth and value. Sadly, she didn't even realize it.

Sometimes you have to know when to let things go, even though you may think you are right. If you always have to win, then that makes you the only champion in your house. If you never let your spouse or your children win a debate or even a simple game on the

Wii, you're creating a spirit of defeat within them. Eventually, your family will just quit trying and lose that passion to win.

I want to surround myself with winners because a winning environment helps everyone rise higher. I have learned that I don't have to win every discussion with Joel because ultimately, if he wins, I win. We're a team and we share each other's victory. That's how you have to see the situation when your mind is screaming, "I want to be right!"

Another way to create a winning atmosphere is to team up with your spouse and those who are close to you in order to help their dreams become reality. Sometimes you can't just encourage them with your words; you have to encourage them with your actions and show your willingness to work toward accomplishing the goal. I knew a woman who was trying to encourage her husband by always saying, "You are going to make a million dollars!" Although she was trying to speak faith into his heart and encourage him, day after day, those words felt like pressure to him. She completely put the burden on his shoulders, and he was overwhelmed with the heavy load.

Anytime I encouraged Joel that we could do something in our lives, I was right there with him, willing to do my part. If we had a financial goal, I did my part to save money. If we were remodeling a house, I was in the yard, laying sod. When we were building a home, I was there every day to meet the subcontractors and help keep us on schedule. When he became pastor of the church, I did my part in the service, too! Joel and I are a team, and the best way I know to show my support for him is to roll up my sleeves right along with him.

I encourage you today to create a winning atmosphere in your home and build champions in the people around you. Don't just put the load of responsibilities for your happiness on your spouse or loved ones. Make the decision to do your part and lift their spirits. Success breeds success, and when you encourage others in their dreams, you are not only building great relationships but you are also setting the stage to bring your own goals and dreams to pass—and that's a win/win situation any way you look at it!

Scripture Reading: 2 Corinthians 10:12–18

⟳~~~⟲   PRAYER FOR TODAY   ⟳~~~⟲

Heavenly Father, today I commit my relationships to You. Help me to create a winning atmosphere in my home, at work, and everywhere I go. Show me how I can help encourage others in their dreams and goals. Thank You for equipping me for every good work by the power of love in me. In Jesus' Name. Amen.

Praying for Your Family

*The prayer of a righteous person
is powerful and effective.*

James 5:16 (NIV)

It's so important to take time to pray every day, especially for your family—your immediate family, your extended family, and even your church family. Every person in your family has been given to you by God. They may not always act right; they may not always treat you right; they may not say the right things all the time, but we still have a responsibility to lift them up in prayer. Even if the relationship is not where it needs to be, God can use your prayers to turn things around.

I know sometimes family relationships can be the most difficult. There can be pain, hurt, and offense; but when you pray, you are opening the door for God's healing in your life and in your family relationships. God doesn't want you to go through life carrying a load of heartache and offense. He doesn't want us to be prisoners of pain. I talk to so many people who have been hurt by family members—someone walked out on them, a child's not living the right way—but I want you to know that if you want to be free, you have to begin to pray past the pain. Luke 6:28 tells us to bless those who curse us and pray for those who mistreat us. When we do the right thing, even when the wrong thing is happening, God will turn things around for our good and bless us beyond our wildest dreams.

I want to encourage you today: when you feel that unction in your heart to pray for a family member, don't ignore it, even if you haven't talked to them in years. Maybe they just came to mind out of the blue. That's the Holy Spirit prompting you to pray. You never know what may be going on in their life, and your prayer may be the prayer that changes everything. The prayer of the righteous is powerful, and as a believer in Jesus, God wants to use your prayers in a mighty way!

Remember, God loves you so much today. He wants to restore you. He wants to restore your family. He has a great future planned for you. Stand in faith, keep believing, and keep praying because there's nothing too difficult for Him. Even if you don't feel like it, take a step of faith; God sees your obedience to Him. He'll honor you because you've honored His Word.

Don't give up even if something is taking longer than you thought; God is a faithful God and He is working behind the scenes on your behalf.

Scripture Reading: 1 Thessalonians 5:16–28

 PRAYER FOR TODAY

Heavenly Father, today I commit to praying for my family. I pray first that they will come to know You in a close, personal way. I pray blessing over them: strength, peace, and wisdom. I choose to forgive those who have wronged me and invite You to do a healing work in my family. In Jesus' Name. Amen.

Chapter Eleven

Receiving Love

His Arms Are Open to You

*"But while he was still a long way off,
his father saw him and was filled with
compassion for him; he ran to his son,
threw his arms around him and kissed him."*
Luke 15:20 (NIV)

I n this day and age, the word "love" can be used in just about any context. We "love" our families or soul mates, and we also "love" a good movie or pizza! It's no wonder people get so confused about the subject of love. One thing is certain: Every person on this earth was created with a deep longing to give and receive love. We develop our personal definition of love by how we were raised and what we saw modeled in our homes growing up. Whether people realize it or not, most have a picture of God in their minds based on what their relationship was like with their natural father. If their earthly father was kind and supportive, they find it easy to see God the same way. On the other hand, if their earthly father was unavailable or distant, they may find it difficult to see the unconditional love that God so freely gives.

I grew up in a home where the phrase "I love you" was as natural as the word "hello." I realize that it's easy for me to accept God's love because of the way I was raised. My parents were always good to me and showed me their unconditional love and approval. But there were occasions when I had to learn to embrace that love . . . like when I knew I did something was wrong—a very rare occasion, of course!

I can remember when I was sixteen years old, my dad would allow me to drive the family car to the grocery store. "Go straight to the store, get the groceries, and then come straight back home," he would say. "Don't pick up any of your friends, just go, and come straight back."

One day, as I was headed for the store, my dad cautioned me, "Victoria, the passenger-side window is off its track. Please don't open the passenger-side door, and especially don't lower the passenger-side window. I have an appointment to get it repaired, but for right now, just don't lower it."

"Okay, Dad," I said with a kiss and a smile as I headed out the door. And as any good, sixteen-year-old girl would do, I went straight to my best friend's house, picked her up, and we headed to the store together. Being the responsible young lady that I was, I told her to be careful about the window. Well, we had barely driven one block when we saw a boy we knew from school walking down the street. Of course, we weren't *trying* to impress him or anything, we just wanted to innocently say hi.

"Just go ahead and roll down the window and say hello to him," I told my friend.

"But I thought your dad said not to," my friend hedged.

Caught up in the moment, and feeling so grown up because I was driving, I said, "Oh, it will be okay. Just do it slowly."

My friend rolled down the window, and we said hello to the boy from school, waving and acting so mature. He seemed so impressed that I was driving, and my friend and I acted as cool as could be. We were so proud of ourselves! Everything was great until my friend started to raise the window. Suddenly it seemed like the world stopped, as I watched the window crack and shatter into a million pieces! I would have given anything to turn back the clock at that moment.

"Oh, no!" I cried. "You have to come home with me and help me explain to my dad what happened," I told my friend. Suddenly the groceries didn't seem so important anymore and we drove straight back home in complete silence. The walk up our driveway wasn't nearly long enough, as I tried to figure out how to explain to my dad what just happened. I walked inside, along with my friend—the one who wasn't supposed to be with me. My dad was in the kitchen making some hamburgers, when he turned and saw us. You can imagine the puzzled look on his face. "Dad, I'm so sorry . . ." I started to say, barely knowing how to explain what had happened.

Because I knew my father loved me, I had the confidence to tell him the whole story, and the moment I admitted to my dad that I had disobeyed, he forgave me. Of course he was disappointed, but he never ceased to love me. In fact, his love for me was just as strong after that incident as before. Our relationship continued to flourish as it does to this day.

Maybe you weren't raised in a family like mine, and it's hard for you to believe that God is so forgiving. Maybe it's time for you to "redefine" what you know as love. Know today that God's love goes way beyond any human love you've ever experienced. He is always patient and kind, always just and forgiving. He weeps when you weep and laughs when you laugh. You are His delight, and He longs to have a loving relationship with you. You bring joy to His heart, and I know He is smiling on you right now as you read these words.

It doesn't matter how many times you've made a mistake; it doesn't matter how many times you've blown it. God is always ready to receive you with open, loving arms. Imagine Him in front of you right now with His arms outstretched, ready to welcome you. Don't run away from Him; run toward Him. Simply take a step of faith to embrace His love and forgiveness today.

Scripture Reading: Luke 15:11–32

PRAYER FOR TODAY

Father God, thank You for loving me and forgiving me today. Thank You for receiving me into Your open arms. Wrap me in Your peace and joy and wash me clean of every stain from the past. Show me Your ways, show me Your love, and help me understand Your goodness. Keep me close to You always. In Jesus' Name. Amen.

You Matter to God

How precious are your thoughts about me, O God.
They cannot be numbered! I can't even count
them; they outnumber the grains of sand!
Psalm 139:17–18 (NLT)

Have you ever wondered what God thinks about, what is on His mind? It says in Psalms that God is mindful *of us*. That means God is constantly thinking about you and me. Many people think God is looking down on them waiting for them to mess up. They say things like, "If I walk into that church, the roof will cave in!" But God's not thinking about your mistakes, failures, or shortcomings. No, His thoughts toward you are good. He's not thinking about what you did wrong, He's thinking about what you did right. He's not thinking about how far you have to go; He's thinking about how far you've come.

Know today that God approves of you. He's pleased with you. He may not be pleased with all your choices or some of the things you do, but when God looks at you, He's not looking at your actions; He's looking at His creation. You are His masterpiece and He's looking at you through His loving and gracious eyes. You matter to God and every detail of your life matters to Him. He counts every hair on your head and bottles every tear that you've cried. You are significant, your life is significant, and the things that concern you, concern Him. He carefully watches over every detail of your life, and there is nothing too big and nothing too small for His attention.

In this day and age, people are considered to be important for so many different reasons—titles, positions, possessions, where you go, what you drive. But God's value system is very different. If you've ever thought that God has too many other "important" things on His plate to be concerned about you and your life, know this today: You are God's number one priority. And there's nothing you can do to be *more* important or *less* important to Him. God values you simply because He created you. You are precious to Him and your value will never change.

God wants you to know how important you are to Him. You are the apple of His eye, the center of His world! He wants you to know His heart of compassion and forgiveness. In fact, all throughout history, people have said things about God, but I believe that what He says about Himself is what's most important. In the book of Exodus, He says that He is a gracious God. He wants you to know that He is compassionate and slow to anger, rich in love. He says that He is forgiving and wants to bless you and your family. He wants you to know that He loves you so much and that He is a jealous God. In other words, He wants your whole heart and He doesn't want to share it with anyone or anything else! He loves you with an everlasting love, and He doesn't want anything to stand in between you and Him.

Today, I encourage you to receive God's love in a new way. Ask Him to help you understand His unconditional love. When you understand His true love, you'll be set free from any kind of inferiority and insecurity. You become more grounded and better able to love others. The more we accept God's love, the more love we will have to give—both to Him and to the people who matter the most to us.

Remember, you are important to God and He is mindful of you today. No matter what cares or concerns you may have, you can take them to Him. He loves to hear you call upon Him and He is waiting to show Himself strong on your behalf.

Scripture Reading: Psalm 139:1–18

PRAYER FOR TODAY

Father in Heaven, thank you for loving me today. Thank You for making me the apple of Your eye. I open my heart to You today and cast every care on You. I keep my heart and mind on You because I know that You are mindful of me and have a good plan in store for my future. In Jesus' Name, Amen.

The Foundation for Confidence

*This is how love is made complete among us
so that we will have confidence on the day of
judgment: In this world we are like Jesus.*

1 John 4:17 (NIV)

S tudies show that children grow and flourish when they are approved, accepted, and valued. But when a child is raised in an environment that is harsh and disapproving, when he feels like he can't be "good enough," his self-esteem is limited.

A survey done for a national magazine revealed that 59 percent of CEOs are firstborn children. I don't find this surprising when you consider how most firstborn children are treated by their parents—everything those children do is so amazing! That first smile, that first word, that first step—each "first" is seen as the most magnificent event of the year. Even most grandparents marvel at and encourage every move of that firstborn child. That constant recognition of every small achievement builds confidence and security.

Did you know God sees you the same way? Regardless of whether you were the firstborn in your family or not, you are the apple of God's eye. He will always treat you like His most valuable child. He applauds you every time you take a step of faith. He's always speaking encouraging words into your heart, saying, "You can rise higher. You can do all things. You can fulfill your destiny."

Let those words sink into your heart, and allow them to build confidence in you. When you understand and receive God's love and encouragement, it will empower you to do more than you ever thought possible. Because of God's love and constant support, you can wake up every day with an attitude of faith and expectancy knowing that He has victory in store for you. You don't have to live feeling guilty or condemned, or like you don't measure up. You may have made some mistakes, but just like a parent helps a child who is learning to walk, God will help you get right back up anytime you fall. Do your part, and instead of dwelling on all you've done wrong in the past, just imagine God smiling down on you. It's very freeing to say, "God is pleased with me. God approves me." Embrace these words and let them create a foundation of confidence in your life.

When you allow God's love to build confidence in you, it enables you to love yourself and love others better. When Jesus walked the earth, He left us two simple commands: Love God and love your neighbor *as you love yourself.* Notice it doesn't just say, "Love God and people." No, it says love others *as* you love yourself. That means you can never love anyone until you have the confidence to love yourself. Loving yourself is not about being selfish; it's about receiving God's love and honoring His creation . . . *you!*

Remember, you are God's most prized possession, the apple of His eye! Be confident in Him and trust that He is at work in your life. Let His love build confidence so that you can boldly embrace every promise and every blessing He has in store for you!

Scripture Reading: Romans 8:28–39

PRAYER FOR TODAY

Heavenly Father, thank You for the gift of Your love which strengthens me, changes me, and builds confidence in me. I receive Your love today and invite You to have Your way in my heart. Help me to love others better as I learn to love myself the way You love me. In Jesus' Name. Amen.

Rest Secure in His Love

Let the beloved of the LORD rest secure in him,
for he shields him all day long, and the one the
LORD loves rests between his shoulders.
Deuteronomy 33:12 (NIV)

God loves you so much today. He wants to lift your burdens and give you rest, security, and confidence in His love. Today's verse says, "the one the LORD loves rests between His shoulders." This paints such a beautiful picture of the invitation for us to just lay our heads on His chest and allow Him to shield us from anything that would come against us in this life.

When we rest securely in His unconditional love, it strengthens us and enables us to enjoy the love of our family, friends, and spouse more—even when their love fails to meet our expectations. When you stand strong in His love, you won't be shaken when the love of others seems uncertain or when you feel like you've let others down.

Joel and I have been married for more than twenty-two years, and the strength of our relationship comes from knowing that God loves us, and even though we may not do everything perfectly, we extend that unconditional love and acceptance to each other. We don't just love each other when things are good or just when we agree on everything; we are committed to loving each other no matter what. That certainly doesn't mean that every day is perfect. There are those days when we don't meet each other's expectations. But when things don't go the right way and I'm tempted to get down on myself, I don't focus on what I've done; I focus on what I know—that I am loved unconditionally and that love carries me through.

We have to remember to find rest and security in the foundation of love in our relationships. We can find stability in knowing that because God loves us, we are empowered to overcome every obstacle in this life. I know I am strongest when I build my days on the foundation of His love for me. I know His love has no limits, and trust that His love will make up the difference when human love falls short.

In the same way that we find security in love, we should offer security to others with our love, too. We should "set the table" for love, so to speak, by allowing words of affirmation to flow freely and creating an atmosphere of love in our homes. We should be comfortable both saying and hearing, "I love you."

I know Joel loves me, but I still like to hear him say it on a regular basis. Sure, they are just three little words, but I allow those words to sink deep into my heart every time I hear them. I know that when I embrace those words, they establish a treasure of security and trust in my heart. I rely on Joel's love and allow it to flood my being, because in any good relationship love has to be the anchor that keeps you steady when the storms of life come.

One time, a young woman heard me speaking on this subject and wrote to tell me how much she appreciated my encouragement to embrace those words "I love you." "I really want to embrace my husband's love," she said, "but I get so down on myself and feel like I'm not good enough for my husband. I feel like I'm apologizing to him all the time and don't measure up to what he needs." She admitted that her personal feelings of inadequacy were driving a wedge in their relationship. In her mind, their relationship was stuck and not progressing the way she felt it should. She knew her husband loved her, but she couldn't embrace his love or allow it to build security in her heart. It was as if she couldn't get beyond her own mistakes and her fear that her husband would reject her. He truly loved her, but she couldn't receive his love. It wasn't until she adjusted her own thinking and let down her defenses that their relationship was rescued from that rut and began progressing toward renewed love and security.

The same thing happens in our relationship with God. When we don't receive His love, it causes us to get stuck. That's why we have to keep ourselves open to Him, and let Him change us from the inside out. We should always remember that God's love is not *based* on our performance, but when we recognize and embrace His love, it will *improve* our performance.

Today, find security and confidence in God's love. Let Him build confidence in you. Choose to let go of misconceptions of the past and trust that His love is perfect. Let Him free you to love others in a new way as you receive His love and rest securely in Him.

Scripture Reading: Psalm 36:5–12

 PRAYER FOR TODAY

Father God, thank You for Your grace and love for me today. I receive Your invitation to rest securely in Your arms. Help to create an atmosphere of love and acceptance for the people in my life. Thank You for causing me to rise higher and higher as I yield myself to You. In Jesus' Name. Amen.

Living Free

Therefore, there is now no condemnation
for those who are in Christ Jesus.
Romans 8:1 (NIV)

In the New Testament, there's a story about a woman who was caught in the act of adultery. The religious leaders had already condemned her in their minds, and their law said she should be stoned. Out of curiosity, they brought her to Jesus to see what He would do, and Jesus surprised them all with His response. Instead of condemning the woman, like they all expected, Jesus showed love and compassion to her. In fact, He turned the whole situation around when He said to the crowd, "You who are without sin, throw the first stone" (see John 8:1–11). The woman's accusers left one by one. Jesus turned to the woman and said, "Where are your accusers? Did anyone condemn you?" She answered, "No one, Lord." Then, Jesus said something very profound, something that gives us insight into who He really is: "Neither do I condemn you. Go and sin no more." God was, in essence, saying, "I don't put my stamp of approval on condemnation. That's not what I'm about." This story clearly shows us that God is not in the business of condemning people; He's in the business of improving and loving people.

Maybe you've encountered people who want to accuse you and "throw stones" at you, but that's not the way our God is. He's never going to throw rocks at you or try to push you down. He wants to empower you to live a better life. Maybe you've made some mistakes, or maybe you've been hurt by someone who threw rocks at you. Today is your day to let go of that hurt and open your heart to receive God's love and forgiveness.

Remember, as long as we live, there will be accusing voices. The faultfinders and rock throwers will always be there. When the negative voices come, we can either believe them and stay stuck in condemnation or we can be free and believe that we're forgiven, accepted, and approved by God. It's up to us to cast the deciding vote for either freedom or condemnation; faith or fear; love or bitterness. Decide today to receive God's love. As you learn to receive His love, not only will you love your life more, but you'll have plenty of love to give away.

My prayer for you today is that you will understand your value and truly see what you have to offer others. Life is too short and too precious to waste a single moment in fear and condemnation. Instead, take captive every negative thought and choose to dwell on the truth of God's Word. Place your hope and confidence in Him so you can live in His everlasting freedom.

Scripture Reading: John 8:1-11

 PRAYER FOR TODAY

Father in Heaven, thank You for Your truth that sets me free. I choose to believe Your Word that says I am free from condemnation in You. I receive Your love, invite You to wash me and make me new. Fill me with Your peace and joy as I keep my mind stayed on You. In Jesus' Name. Amen.

Say "Yes" to Love

Therefore, if anyone is in Christ,
he is a new creation; old things have passed away;
behold, all things have become new.
2 *Corinthians 5:17 (NKJV)*

There was a man in the Bible named Nicodemus who asked Jesus, "What is this new birth I keep hearing about? What does it mean to be born again? How can a person enter their mother's womb a second time?" Jesus answered him by explaining that it's your spirit that is reborn and made alive. Romans 10:9–10 tells us that we are born again when we say yes to Jesus.

When you say yes to Jesus, when you receive Him as your Lord and Savior, you immediately become new and alive in your spirit. You are cleansed of all sin and all unrighteousness, and God's Spirit makes His home inside of you. It's as if God takes the DNA of a sinner out of you and puts the DNA of a saint in its place. You're not programmed to sin anymore; in fact, it becomes difficult to live the same old way because now you are programmed to say yes to Jesus.

Saying yes to Jesus isn't a one-time thing. We have to wake up every morning and choose to say yes to Him in our minds, in our attitudes, and in our actions. We have to say yes to His Word and come into agreement with His promises. In the same way you exercise and feed your body every day in order to grow and be strong, you have to exercise and feed your spirit if you want it to grow and produce the great things that God has deposited on the inside of you.

I encourage you today, if there's any area of your life that's been closed to God, open your heart and say yes to Him today. He loves you with an everlasting love, and He has a wonderful plan for your future. Don't waste another second of your life holding on to fear, doubt, or regret. Say yes to Him in every area of your life and let Him transform you and lead you into the abundant, everlasting life He has prepared for you!

Scripture Reading: John 3:1–18

 PRAYER FOR TODAY

Father God, today I say yes to You. I say yes to Your work in my life. I say yes to You in my mind, will, and emotions. I receive Your love fresh and new and surrender every area of my heart to You. Thank You for choosing me and equipping me for every good work You have in store for me. In Jesus' Name. Amen.

About the Author

Victoria Osteen has always had an infectious passion and enthusiasm for life. A native Houstonian, Victoria began her career in her family's jewelry business and now works with the most precious treasure of all—people. She is an inspiration to and mentor of women everywhere as she ministers alongside her husband, Joel, setting a wonderful example for their two children, Jonathan and Alexandra. Victoria is active in her community and committed to helping women, children, and families discover their purpose and reach their highest potential.

Visit Victoria's website at www.victoriaosteen.com.

Printed in the United States
By Bookmasters